921   429882

Keates, Jonathan
William III &
Mary II

CHARTER OAK MIDDLE SCHOOL
280 POINDEXTER AVENUE
MOORPARK, CA 93021

Penguin Monarchs

THE HOUSES OF WESSEX AND DENMARK

Athelstan	Tom Holland
Aethelred the Unready	Richard Abels
Cnut	Ryan Lavelle
Edward the Confessor	James Campbell

THE HOUSES OF NORMANDY, BLOIS AND ANJOU

William I	Marc Morris
William II	John Gillingham
Henry I	Edmund King
Stephen	Carl Watkins
Henry II	Richard Barber
Richard I	Thomas Asbridge
John	Nicholas Vincent

THE HOUSE OF PLANTAGENET

Henry III	Stephen Church
Edward I	Andy King
Edward II	Christopher Given-Wilson
Edward III	Jonathan Sumption
Richard II	Laura Ashe

THE HOUSES OF LANCASTER AND YORK

Henry IV	Catherine Nall
Henry V	Anne Curry
Henry VI	James Ross
Edward IV	A. J. Pollard
Edward V	Thomas Penn
Richard III	Rosemary Horrox

THE HOUSE OF TUDOR

Henry VII	Sean Cunningham
Henry VIII	John Guy
Edward VI	Stephen Alford
Mary I	John Edwards
Elizabeth I	Helen Castor

THE HOUSE OF STUART

James I	Thomas Cogswell
Charles I	Mark Kishlansky
[Cromwell	David Horspool]
Charles II	Clare Jackson
James II	David Womersley
William III & Mary II	Jonathan Keates
Anne	Richard Hewlings

THE HOUSE OF HANOVER

George I	Tim Blanning
George II	Norman Davies
George III	Amanda Foreman
George IV	Stella Tillyard
William IV	Roger Knight
Victoria	Jane Ridley

THE HOUSES OF SAXE-COBURG & GOTHA AND WINDSOR

Edward VII	Richard Davenport-Hines
George V	David Cannadine
Edward VIII	Piers Brendon
George VI	Philip Ziegler
Elizabeth II	Douglas Hurd

JONATHAN KEATES

William III and Mary II

Partners in Revolution

ALLEN LANE
an imprint of
PENGUIN BOOKS

ALLEN LANE

UK | USA | Canada | Ireland | Australia
India | New Zealand | South Africa

Allen Lane is part of the Penguin Random House group of companies
whose addresses can be found at global.penguinrandomhouse.com.

First published 2015
001

Copyright © Jonathan Keates, 2015

The moral right of the author has been asserted

Set in 9.5/13.5 pt Sabon LT Std
Typeset by Jouve (UK), Milton Keynes
Printed in Great Britain by Clays Ltd, St Ives plc

ISBN: 978–0–141–97687–7

Contents

Introduction

It is a Saturday afternoon at the London Library. The issue hall is almost empty, the reading room, so busy earlier in the week, today contains only a handful of dedicated researchers and an agreeably sepulchral quiet pervades the stacks and staircases. Outside, the kind of autumn day described by that eloquent Scots monosyllable 'dreich' – dark, cold and damp – hangs over St James's Square. None of us at our desks, with our iPads, pens, sheaves of lined A4 and little mounds of printed wisdom plucked from the shelves, has any idea of what is about to disturb the peace of communal scholarship. Neither have the four or five readers dozing over learned journals in the semicircle of red armchairs.

From out of the afternoon streets south of the square arises a sound which insists that we sit up and take proper notice of the occasion. It is the music of an Ulster Protestant marching band – not one, in fact, but several, converging with inexorable shrillness and precision on the green, fenced space, its plane trees still in leaf. Some of us move sheepishly to the window, ashamed to admit to anything so vulgar as mere curiosity.

The roadway is soon filled with a procession headed by files of smartly uniformed boys and girls trilling fifes and beating drums with a combination of expert nonchalance

and focused intensity. There is a sudden halt to these mar-
tial strains, as a man in a bowler hat, his orange sash more
elaborate than those worn by the band members, steps forward, apparently to address somebody concealed by the
greenery behind the railings. A profound, almost desperate
respect seizes the listeners. When at last he raises his hat,
there are rousing cheers and cries of 'God save the queen!',
then the fluting and drumming resumes and the procession
marches smartly off in its tangerine segments towards
Regent Street. Aware that the library will close in an hour
or so, we return, however reluctantly, to our desks.

Some of us watching the ceremony in the square will by
now have made the connection between place, date and
celebrants. In two days' time it will be the fourth of November, the birthday of the man who, for these marchers and
musicians, is still 'the Deliverer', gallant champion of their
liberties, guarantor of their freedom of worship, their
saviour from bigotry and persecution. It is entirely in
accordance with his personal dislike of the showmanship
and public display demanded of royalty that the statue of
King William III should be hidden from view in one of
central London's leafiest and least-frequented public spaces.
Equally characteristic of posterity's attitude towards him is
the fact that this memorial should have fetched up here by
accident, almost a century after his death.

The sculptor John Bacon, whose son finished it off, used
a fancy portrait by Godfrey Kneller as the model for his
presentation of William as a Roman general, complete with
cuirass, buskins and laurel wreath. From canvas to bronze
the Bacons transferred the king's unforgettable profile,

lantern-jawed, hook-nosed, keen-eyed, the countenance of a monarch for whom being royal meant more than sitting for portraits and wearing the right clothes. They've taken trouble, too, with the horse. Short in the withers, wide in the rump, with a curly mane and a tail like a fan, this is evidently one of those Spanish steeds so favoured by cavalry commanders on the European battlefields of the seventeenth century.

Apart from a statue in the Central Criminal Court, not readily on show to the general public, London boasts no sculptural likeness of William's consort – crowned queen in her own right as Mary II – not even at Kensington Palace, where she died of smallpox in 1694, aged only thirty-two. The single effigy of her which exists elsewhere occupies one of two niches on the High Street facade of Oxford's University College. In the other, brandishing an arm from which the sceptre has long disappeared, is the once-loved sister with whom she quarrelled bitterly and who eventually succeeded William III as Queen Anne. Almost nobody waiting at the bus stops across the street is likely to know anything of Mary and her gloomy, asthmatic Dutch husband, let alone of the momentous upheaval which made them joint sovereigns in 1689. Among kings and queens whose names underpin the unique continuity of England's historical narrative over the nine centuries between William the Conqueror and Elizabeth II, William and Mary rank among the least glamorous, quickly ignored after their deaths and enshrined in popular memory only by the fact that they were our only king and queen who, by an accident of politics, shared the throne.

Their one chance of gaining popular attention was miserably fudged (on purpose, some might say) by those who had the opportunity in their gift. The year 1988 marked the tercentenary of the Glorious Revolution, a moment of genuine significance in the history of the United Kingdom. It was the completion of a sequence of events, involving civil war, the defeat of monarchical absolutism and the assertion of fundamental freedoms, which would subsequently inspire the leaders of revolution in America and France and the evolution of a modern political culture based on popular representation that would be imitated, adopted or desired throughout the entire world. Among Britain's positive contributions to the benefit of humankind – of which there are rather more than Britons nowadays are prepared to acknowledge – this democratic template is arguably the most valuable and enduring.

We should therefore have been celebrating 1688 and the reign of William and Mary with something more than fifes, drums, orange sashes and bowler hats. Nineteen eighty-eight, after all, was the high-water mark of Thatcherism, with its triumphal emphasis on Britain's significance as an international beacon of liberty. The prime minister herself had become evangelical in this cause. The following year saw her quite rightly reminding the French, celebrating the bicentenary of 'liberté, égalité, fraternité', that England had done all that sort of thing a century earlier and that the 'Déclaration des droits de l'homme et du citoyen' had its intellectual origins in the Declaration of Rights accepted by King William on 13 February 1689.

So why was 1688–1988 such a spectacular non-event?

The tercentenary went unmarked by a major exhibition at the British Museum or anywhere else. A pity, since the visual and decorative aspects of William and Mary's reign are of major importance, as Hampton Court, Kensington Palace and Greenwich Royal Hospital all bear witness. No thanksgiving service took place at Westminster for the event whose impact permanently established Parliament's supremacy in the government of the realm and confirmed the rights of every subject under the rule of law. No parades down Whitehall celebrated the creation, as a result of the European conflict into which William led the nation during the 1690s, of the modern British armed forces. You might have thought that this last aspect, at least, would have found favour with patriots of whatever political colour. Not even a commemorative series of postage stamps acknowledged the tercentenary. A scattering of academic conferences took place, mostly in the Netherlands, justifiably proud of its role in ensuring the Revolution's strategic success, but this was all.

It did not help William and Mary's cause that British historians of the 1980s included a distinctly heretical echelon of Tory revisionists, who believed the Glorious Revolution's effects to have been wildly overrated, dismissing it as an episode which had briefly troubled the waters of a profound conservatism forming the genuine core of national life. They saw no profit in marking an episode which, by its very nature, seemed to embody all they loathed in the shape of consensus, compromise and progress. The fact that the Revolution, in design and intention, had embodied the ultimate conservative credo of wanting things to change so that they can stay as they are, a principle successfully grasped at a later historical period by their hero Benjamin Disraeli, seems to have eluded the Tory party-poopers of 1988.

Thus William and Mary lost their slot, as it were, in that recognition of shared historical experience which ought to form part of any nation's sense of identity. Almost three decades later, they are in still greater danger of oblivion, given that history is not a compulsory element of the national curriculum and is presented via random episodes rather than as a narrative sequence within a chronological framework. Britain's joint sovereigns, along with their era, have been relegated to that rapidly deepening pool of shadow which, for most of us, now envelops English history.

Monarchs do not create the cultural identity of their reigns single-handedly. For example, what we loosely term 'the Restoration' depended for its mood and tone on a great many other factors besides the priapic itches – or inches – of the restored King Charles II. Thus we do not owe the beginnings of our present constitutional settlement, commercial culture and civil society exclusively to William and Mary. The 1690s are crucial to the evolution of modern England in ways which neither monarch could have appreciated.

Yet it is precisely because of who each of them was, of how they together encompassed the dauntingly complex task of reigning over England under the unique circumstances which brought them to the crown, and because of the cool head and single-mindedness of William especially, in harnessing the nation's destiny to his own personal imperatives, that the kingdom of 1702, the year he died, looked a significantly different country from the one they had jointly taken over a mere fourteen years previously. Without any private or stated intention of doing so, William and Mary repositioned the English monarchy in its relation to the executive and the people in ways which ensured its survival, both as an instrument of government and as a unifying emblem of continuity. As grandchildren of King Charles I, their achievement was to guarantee that none of their successors would end as a headless corpse on a public scaffold. If the roles of king and queen, not to speak of the court life surrounding them, experienced a diminishing significance in the life of the nation, this was all to the good. By the end of the reign, Britain had assumed the outlines of that modern society, based on liberty, property and legitimate aspiration, which has since been adopted throughout the world. Such a model was not the sole creation of William and Mary, but it could certainly not have been achieved without them.

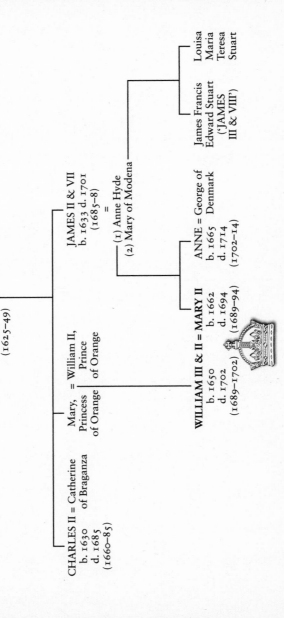

CHARLES I = Henrietta Maria
b. 1600   of France
d. 1649
(1625–49)

CHARLES II = Catherine
b. 1630   of Braganza
d. 1685
(1660–85)

Mary, = William II,
Princess   Prince
of Orange of Orange

JAMES II & VII
b. 1633 d. 1701
(1685–8)
=
(1) Anne Hyde
(2) Mary of Modena

WILLIAM III & II = MARY II
b. 1650   b. 1662
d. 1702   d. 1694
(1689–1702)   (1689–94)

ANNE = George of
b. 1665   Denmark
d. 1714
(1702–14)

James Francis
Edward Stuart
('JAMES
III & VIII')

Louisa
Maria
Teresa
Stuart

William III and Mary II

I
Children of State

Let's start with Shakespeare. From birth William and Mary were each destined to fulfil the role outlined in *Hamlet* by Laertes for Ophelia's benefit, when it looks as though she may have her eye on the eponymous Prince of Denmark for a husband.

> His greatness weighed, his will is not his own;
> For he himself is subject to his birth.
> He may not, as unvalued persons do,
> Carve for himself; for on his choice depends
> The safety and the health of this whole state;
> And therefore must his choice be circumscribed
> Unto the voice and yielding of that body
> Whereof he is the head.[1]

In their different ways, William, Prince of Orange, and Mary, Princess of York, were victims of their birth, hostages, like every other prince and princess in an age of profound dynastic calculations, to the fate prescribed for them by their parents or by manipulative politicians. Each was what was then known as 'a child of state', whose family life and domestic contentment depended exclusively on plans made by others as to whom they should marry. Such decisions were based on national advantage rather than on anything so trifling as personal inclination or prospective happiness.

That William and Mary were both half Stuart was a further potential misfortune. The myth-history of Britain developed over many centuries has successfully wreathed this Scottish dynasty in an impenetrable web of nostalgia and romance. Far too much is forgiven King Charles I on account of his art collection, his skill on the bass viol and the undeniable fact that 'He nothing common did or mean'[2] when facing his executioners in 1649. We love King Charles II, 'the Merry Monarch', still more, amid his mistresses, spaniels, yachts and racehorses, despite his cynical egoism, his ruthless sacrifice of friends and loyal ministers and his cold-blooded willingness to cut a deal with King Louis XIV whereby, in exchange for ready cash, England was effectively sold to France. As for the family's last hurrah in the shape of Young Pretender Charles Edward Stuart, Bonnie Prince Charlie, just how many shortbread tins and yards of tartan does it take to create a legend?

A more detached scrutiny of the Stuarts suggests that, for William and Mary, this shared gene was something of a *damnosa hereditas*. Their personal triumph lay in successfully avoiding those serious flaws of character and errors of judgement which characterized the royal house at its worst. Pig-headed obstinacy and refusal to face facts, an overweening sense of regal entitlement and a failure to grasp the importance of mutuality in the relationship between sovereign and subject – all of these traits, exhibited with so little restraint by other members of their family, were by sheer good fortune absent in these two children of state.

This seems more miraculous when we consider just how marked such characteristics were in each of their Stuart parents. William's mother was Princess Mary of England, daughter of King Charles I, who had been married in 1641, at the age of nine, to the Dutch prince Willem of Orange-Nassau. The match was one of expediency, since Charles and his French Catholic queen, Henrietta Maria, saw obvious benefits in cultivating an alliance with the Protestant Netherlands, whose money and munitions would aid the royal cause in its coming struggle with Parliament. The Dutch, in their loose republican confederation known as the United Provinces, headed by Willem's father, Frederick Henry, as 'stadholder', viewed the marriage as a chance to detach England from a potential alliance with Spain, from whose grip they had themselves broken away sixty years earlier.

Princess Mary antagonized her husband's compatriots from the moment she arrived at The Hague. In adulthood she remained the proud, spoiled Stuart brat Willem brought home, tactless towards the Dutch, quarrelling with her husband's family, obsessed with her superior rank as daughter and granddaughter of kings British and French, embarrassing English diplomats sent to negotiate with her and outraging Holland's Calvinist sobriety with her passion for hunting, dancing and masquerades.

When Willem himself inopportunely died of smallpox, aged only twenty-four, Mary's vulnerability as his widow became more exposed precisely because of this charmless combination of arrogance and self-indulgence. She was far too narrow-minded to appreciate the significance of the momentous shift in the surrounding political landscape following her father's execution in 1649, with Oliver Cromwell feared or grudgingly respected throughout Europe and what remained of her English royal family skulking in exile. The verdict of two Dutch travellers on a courtesy visit to her while she was staying in Bruges in 1656 says it all: 'The princess received us in her customary manner, that is to say coldly and without saying a word. In the present age this cannot please, however great the prince may be.'[3]

Things were admittedly not made easier for the proud Princess of Orange by the brooding presence of her mother-in-law, a parody of the genre in the person of Amalia von Solms-Braunfels, former lady-in-waiting to King Charles's sister, Elizabeth, Queen of Bohemia. A poor relation of the house of Orange, she was determined to better herself by currying favour among European monarchs with the aim of establishing her family as a marketable princely dynasty. By 1650 this 'most successful social climber of her day',[4] widowed three years previously, had pushed her advantages beyond the expectations of even the most cynical politician. Cardinal Richelieu, in the name of France, had bribed her with diamond earrings, his successor, Cardinal Mazarin, was likewise impressed, while the Spaniards, grateful for her diplomatic manoeuvres in their peace negotiations with the United Provinces, gave her two handsome estates and a sweetener in ready cash.

Marriage of Amalia's unpromising son Willem to Mary

of England was part of a game plan which had already involved disposing of several daughters as brides for powerful German princes. The two women heartily loathed each other from the outset. Mary's role, where Amalia was concerned, was simply to furnish a male heir for the house of Orange as soon as she reached childbearing age and at eighteen, in 1650, she became pregnant. In late October, as she neared her term, Willem fell dangerously ill with smallpox, which carried him off in less than a week, aged only twenty-four. On 4 November, in a black-hung chamber among midwives clad in mourning, his widow gave birth to a moderately healthy boy.

Christened William Henry, he became a child of state on emerging from the womb. It can be said, in truth, that he never had a childhood at all. Even allowing for the haste with which 'hopeful princes', as the seventeenth century called royal heirs of the male sex, were thrust out of infancy into premature adulthood, William's earliest years were some of the loneliest and most sombre among those of his high-born contemporaries. We can make what we choose of the fact that he was an only child, lacking a father and brought up in an atmosphere poisoned by family discord. Like his maternal grandfather, Charles I, he was stunted in growth, with the additional disadvantage of spinal deformity and suffering from asthma attacks which grew more devastating with age. Some of the Italianate handsomeness of his mother's bloodline declared itself in his brilliant black eyes and floridly sensuous mouth, but the effect was ruined for many by a hook nose and a deathly pale complexion. He seldom smiled and the genuine charm and warmth he possessed were shown rarely, to intimate friends and valued advisers. Nobody thought to school him in that most indispensable of royal mysteries, the art of courting popular favour.

Under his mother's guardianship, contested from the outset by his grandmother Amalia, the infant William was paraded, for four hours each day, before visitors to the Binnenhof, the gloomy medieval castle in The Hague where he grew up. At five years old, he began his education with lessons in religion from Cornelis Trigland, an esteemed theologian, who remained his spiritual mentor well into adulthood. William never abandoned his fundamental Calvinist beliefs, based on the doctrine of predestination, which singles out a limited number for salvation, though these remain unaware of such distinction during their earthly lives. This concept of 'election', of being specially favoured by the Almighty, notoriously fosters smugness among evangelical Christians, but this was never counted among William's faults even by those most hostile to him. If he genuinely felt the hand of divine providence, it was in being allowed to fulfil his self-prescribed destiny as leader of a European alliance against the ambitions of a vain, greedy and presumptuous French tyrant.

The impact of this Dutch Protestant value system on the English he came to rule has been underestimated, like almost everything else William of Orange brought them. A major feature of life in the Calvinist Netherlands was a significant degree of tolerance towards other faiths and denominations, something not native to England at that time, however much we now pride ourselves on it as a core aspect of notional 'Englishness'. The United Provinces, more particularly their cities, Amsterdam, Leyden and The Hague, were noted throughout Europe as a refuge, not just for Protestants fleeing Catholic persecution or an increasingly doctrinaire Church of England, but also for Marrano Jews from Spain and Portugal, seeking a place where they could practise their religion unassailed by the inquisitors of the Holy Office. Such distinctively Dutch comprehensiveness was more practical than high-minded, understood as a motor of commercial prosperity, military enterprise and diplomatic ease of manoeuvre. As a monarch needing to rely on the honesty and efficiency of Anglicans, Calvinists, Lutherans, Jews and not a few Catholics from the nations in alliance against France, William would help to shape a new model of European statehood, in which religious differences would no longer be a matter for exile, martyrdom or civil strife.

A more ambiguous moral and spiritual atmosphere altogether surrounded the early years of his English cousin Mary Stuart, born on 30 April 1662 at St James's Palace in London. She was the eldest surviving child of Anne Hyde, whom King Charles II's brother James, Duke of York, had first met at The Hague during his exile, when she was a lady-in-waiting to Princess Mary of Orange. 'Carnally given to women', in the seventeenth-century phrase, James toyed with Anne as a mistress before secretly marrying her while they were both still in Holland. A second wedding ceremony, hardly less hugger-mugger, took place following Charles's restoration in 1660, pressed on the couple by Anne's father, Lord Clarendon, horrified to discover she was pregnant. Diarist Samuel Pepys, gossiping about the affair with his patron, the Earl of Sandwich, tartly recorded: 'my Lord told me that among his father's many old sayings that he had writ in a book of his, this is one: that he that doth get a wench with child and marries her afterward it is as if a man should shit in his hat and then clap it upon his head.'[5]

The infant in question, a boy, died at only a month old. Charles's no-nonsense advice to James to make the best of a bad job consisted of quoting the old English proverb 'You must drink as you have brewed'.[6] The king nevertheless admired Anne, now acknowledged Duchess of York, for her 'great wit and excellent parts',[7] commending her courage and strength of character. All these virtues, together with a certain hard-nosed realism in appraising the slippery court circles now surrounding her, were passed on to her second child, the princess whose birth, according to Pepys, pleased nobody, perhaps because of her mother's lack of royal blood.[8]

As it happened, James was enchanted by little Mary, who became more of a consolation when Duchess Anne, ravaged by breast cancer, worn out by further pregnancies and developing a serious weight problem from overeating as a reaction to his endless infidelities, collapsed at the end of a long supper party and died in delirious agony. The two surviving children – a younger daughter had been named after her – were promptly declared 'children of state', as their father's only legitimate Stuart successors. While the king himself remained without a lawful heir, James stood next in line to the English throne.

At nine years old, Mary was already wise beyond her

years but it was thought prudent to shield her from the one particular aspect of his wife's last hours which must have gladdened the duke. A convert, during his Civil War exile, to Catholicism, he was as zealous and energetic in confessing his sins as in breaking the Sixth Commandment and well on the way towards developing that kind of joyless, blinkered fervour typical of proselytes. Possibly to draw her husband closer to her, Anne herself, some years before she died, embraced his faith, ultimately refusing the Church of England sacrament while on her deathbed. Mary's discovery in adulthood of this apostasy was traumatic enough to stiffen the Protestant conviction with which she herself would in due time face a demise just as untimely.

It was precisely so as to save their lives that the princess and her younger sister, Anne, were hurried away from St James's after their mother's funeral to the healthier air of the rambling Tudor palace of Richmond, where the two girls learned music, dancing and other accomplishments needful for turning them into suitable marriage prospects for European royal families. They took part in plays and masques at their uncle's court, spoke French with foreign diplomats and learned to get on with their spirited Italian stepmother, Maria Beatrice d'Este – 'Mary of Modena' to the English – whom the Duke of York, twenty-five years her senior, had taken as his second wife soon after Anne Hyde's death.

Mary of York's own marital destiny was determined by King Charles II's manoeuvres in the wider sphere of European politics. Between 1664 and 1674, England had fought two wars with the Dutch, each disastrous economically and revealing the incompetence and unpreparedness of the British navy as a fighting force. It was the second of these, beginning in 1672, which saw the twenty-two-year-old Prince William of Orange springing swiftly to prominence as captain-general of Holland's armies against the invading French troops of King Louis XIV, acting in concert with England. Charles's alliance with France had been bought via the promise of an annual subsidy in the squalid secret treaty signed at Dover two years before.

William, capitalizing on a widespread fear that the United Provinces, only recently freed from Spanish dominance, were now about to fall prey to a still stronger Catholic power, allowed himself to become the centrepiece of a highly effective propaganda campaign as the Protestant deliverer leading the beleaguered Calvinist faithful against a Romish Antichrist. The lynching in The Hague, by an enraged mob, of the Dutch republic's pro-French chief minister, Jan de Witt, gave William the chance to figure as Holland's man of the hour, ready to assume a position enjoyed by earlier members of the Orange-Nassau dynasty as a head of state ostensibly without sovereign authority and always respectful of legality, the constitution and the popular will.

This was the first major test of his political career and it was to have an incalculable resonance when, sixteen years later, he seized a similar opportunity, carrying far greater potential, offered him by the affairs of England. His apparent lack of experience, in this coup of 1672, counted for nothing in comparison with his precociously intuitive grasp of motivation and incentive in those closest to him, his gift for harnessing their talents and loyalty, the relentless precision of his capacious memory and the personal sense of mission guiding him in his armed opposition to the bullying self-aggrandizement and territorial acquisitiveness of Louis XIV. William would devote the rest of a short life to this single engrossing project. To his absorption with it Britain owes her transformation, after 1688, into a world power.

Charles II's withdrawal of his navy from the war, following treaty negotiations with the Dutch in the early weeks of 1674, left him better able to be seen as trying to advance the interests of his Protestant nephew against those of his Catholic cousin. His plan was to marry fifteen-year-old Princess Mary of York to William of Orange and the matter was eventually raised by England's envoy to the United Provinces, Sir William Temple. The latter was struck immediately by the unorthodox nature of the prince's attitude. For a start, he asked Temple's opinion 'as a friend, and not as the King's Ambassador'.[9] This mark of respect was typical of someone for whom ceremonious politeness from a social inferior always mattered less than getting an honest answer. More unusual, in a contemporary context, was the value William evidently set on compatibility between a royal husband and wife: 'no circumstances of fortune or interest would engage him, without those of the person, especially those of humour and dispositions ... he would have [a wife] that he thought likely to live well with him, which he thought chiefly depended on her disposition and education.'[10] On these terms, Temple's wife, Dorothy, was given the task of checking out Princess Mary as a likely match.

Despite vigorous opposition from the Duke of York, who

sought Catholic husbands for both his daughters, William invited himself to England in October 1677, journeying from Harwich to Newmarket, where the king was enjoying the racing season. Charles took for granted his nephew's readiness to go through with the marriage as part of the peace settlement ending the Anglo-Dutch enmity and was surprised by William's insistence on meeting Mary before clinching the deal. The pair were formally introduced when the court returned to London, but it was another week before a disgruntled James, accepting the engagement as a fait accompli, announced it to his daughter, 'whereupon her highness wept all that afternoon and the following day'.[11]

The speed with which wedding preparations went forward reflected both William's impatience and Charles's determination to patch up the peace agreement as quickly as possible. '[R]emember,' he warned William, 'that love and war do not agree well together.'[12] Love, at this stage, formed no part of an arrangement from which both uncle and nephew had something to gain politically. Whatever the prince's pre-marital scruples, as earlier expressed to Temple, or his haste in concluding the match, he was not prepared to assume the guise of an ardently romantic suitor. For her part, Mary was the archetypal dynastic victim of international statecraft. An increasing awareness of the realpolitik underlying her hasty betrothal did not improve her mood. National rejoicing at a Protestant royal marriage, with loyal addresses, bonfires and conduits running with wine, was belied by the mixture of froideur and despairing resentment with which the two cousins approached matrimony.

At the ceremony, which took place on 4 November,

William's birthday, in Mary's bedchamber at St James's Palace, King Charles was jokily avuncular, poking his head around the curtains when the pair were safely in bed to cry: 'Now nephew, to your work! Hey St George for England!'[13] Soon afterwards, William retreated to the suite of rooms provided for him in Whitehall Palace and the couple remained apart for the next ten days. William was a good dancer, but at the state ball given on the eve of their departure for Holland, it was noted that he only once took Mary as a partner.

There was nothing in the way of a honeymoon, nor would the bridegroom have known what to do with himself if there had been. Eager to quit England, whose court, with its atmosphere of sleaze, venality and scruffiness, disgusted him, William could at least enjoy the satisfaction of having achieved his object. He had spied out the land, identifying potential supporters while being under no illusions as to how quickly, in most cases, their loyalties might shift, and had grasped the importance of his own position as the son of a Stuart married to a princess of the same family, and now third in line to the English throne. His uncle had no legitimate heirs and his father-in-law, as designated successor, had married a second wife whose pregnancies had so far been unsuccessful. England, for William, was there to be utilized, by whatever means, in his grand scheme of opposition to France and he would stop at nothing in pursuit of this single aim. Fortune, more swiftly than even his superfine intelligence could have divined, stood ready to assist him.

2

The Protestant Wind

There's a sense in which Mary's short lifespan – a mere thirty-two years – seems haunted by her subconscious awareness of the proximity of death. Everything happened to her sooner rather than later, as if in syntony with this intimation of the brief moment allotted. Though her education did not supply the perspectives granted William through an early contact with statesmen, scientists and divines, she was more deeply intuitive, thoughtful and analytical than the conventional good girl into which the collective verdict of historiography has shaped her. There was always more to Mary than Protestant piety and a fondness for knitting, old folk songs and blue and white porcelain. Her natural intelligence was enhanced by that quality the French call *débrouillardise*, the ability of certain people to look out for themselves and make the best of seriously unpromising circumstances. Arriving in the Netherlands, she not only squared up to her new role as consort of the Stadholder of the United Provinces, but set herself the task of learning to love a man whose profound, almost pathological cult of solitariness often made him appear selfish and callous towards her. There was to be no question of an alternative attachment. The evolution, bizarre and unlikely at various stages, of their relationship into a love match has been aptly compared to the story of Beauty and the Beast.

Seventeenth-century princesses were expected to breed and in this, the most important of her duties, Mary was a failure. Following the two miscarriages she suffered in the spring and autumn of 1678, William saw no need to console his wife and seems not to have tried again for an heir. Instead he took one of her English ladies-in-waiting, Elizabeth Villiers, known as 'Squinting Betty', for a mistress, a role she continued to occupy until an access of remorse on William's part, following his wife's death, induced him to dismiss her. Deeply pained, Mary nevertheless waited another six years before confronting her husband with his infidelity and even then seems to have been less concerned for herself than for the moral condition of his soul. Elizabeth, summarily despatched to England, soon came back and Mary, nothing if not philosophical, learned to endure her. Perhaps she reflected that Squinting Betty had done nothing more than honour a family tradition: her great-uncle George, Duke of Buckingham, had been the homosexual love object of King James I, and her cousin Barbara, Lady Castlemaine, was made a duchess in her own right for bedchamber services to King Charles II. In a letter of condolence to a friend whose child had recently died, Mary wrote: 'If one could hinder oneself setting one's heart too much upon those we love, we should be the readier to die.'[1] This single sentence, with its touching confusion of pronouns, speaks volumes about its author.

Mary's two pregnancies, the continuing though always discreet presence of Elizabeth Villiers in William's entourage and his instinctive gallantry and attentiveness to women all tend to discredit the suggestion, often stated as fact, that he was predominantly homosexual. Gilbert Burnet, the Anglican clergyman who gained his confidence during a period of political exile, mentions 'one sort [of vice], in which he was very cautious and secret'.[2] Though this has been made much of by historians and biographers, the allusion here is most probably to the ongoing liaison with *la* Villiers rather than to the love that dared not speak its name.

More persuasive in this respect was the evidence of William's deep attachment, over many years, to two Dutch noblemen, Hans Willem Bentinck, best man at his wedding, whom he later created Duke of Portland, and Arnold Joost van Keppel, made Earl of Albemarle. He was perfectly open in his tenderness towards each of them. In a letter to Bentinck, for example, dated 15 August 1679, he writes: 'It is impossible to tell you with what pain I parted from you this morning, or how distressed I was at leaving you in such a state or what anxiety I am in at the moment. I could not live without you and if ever I felt I loved you it is today.'[3] It was Bentinck who was beside William as he died. Scurrilous gossip, particularly at the French court, talked up the two men's eventual rivalry for their master's favour, transmogrifying each of them, more especially Keppel, strikingly good-looking, into royal *mignons*, but nothing whatever supports this from the testimony of their immediate circle. Most significantly, there is no sign that such mutual devotion made Mary jealous or unhappy.

The love between William and these men was clearly homosocial rather than homosexual, based on his intense

regard for loyalty in those closest to him and on the cama-
raderie engendered by the military environment in which he
felt so much at home. When the United Provinces finally
signed a peace treaty with France at Nijmegen in 1678,
after wars lasting almost a decade, King Louis XIV was
reckoned to have emerged the victor. Battered by the struggle, the Dutch resigned themselves both to his demands and
to his notoriously arbitrary attitude towards keeping an
agreement. William's role as the provinces' stadholder was
still ambiguous. He was the captain-general but not the
sovereign of a nation whose republicanism was essential to
its identity. Nevertheless he had gained a reputation as a
risk-taking military champion, unfailingly courageous in
the field. Even if, throughout his campaigns, William lost
more battles than he won, his personal bravery, commitment and leadership were never in doubt.

There was no question of abandoning his mission simply
because the war was over, and Louis understood this.
Among the latter's notable flaws was the unforgiving nature
of his egoism. Those who challenged his supremacy, refused
to acknowledge his monopoly of public attention or dared,
in whatever sense, to look him in the face were never par-
doned. William rapidly became a target of the king's spiteful
resentment, expressed through French diplomats' attempts
at marginalizing him in their dealings with the Dutch. Louis
overplayed his hand at last by sending troops to invade
and occupy the Provençal city of Orange, a personal fief-
dom of William's family since 1531. The town had served
as a refuge for Huguenots, the French Protestants whom
Louis, now posing as the leader of Catholic Christendom,

was starting to persecute with military raids, known as *dragonnades*, on the areas in which these heretics were concentrated.

William thus had a moral as well as a private imperative to empower his efforts at rallying the Dutch and their potential allies in Germany and Scandinavia against France. Swiftly he mastered the art of compromise with his political opponents in the United Provinces. As William Temple reported, 'He is in perpetual consultation with the most popular of them here (and that were thought his enemies) ... [and] dines every day with the deputies of one town or other, all which, joined to the sense they have what a rascally peace they have made ... has very sensibly increased his authority here.'[4] This willingness to listen to others, to discuss and sift their opinions, became part of William's personal style, crucial to his later dealings with politicians and their parties when he was crowned King of England.

That likelihood drew considerably closer on 7 February 1685, when King Charles II, after a lingering illness, died of a stroke. His brother, the Duke of York, single legitimate heir, succeeded as James II and was duly crowned, alongside his Italian consort, Mary Beatrice, in a Protestant ceremonial at Westminster Abbey after the pair of them had taken care to hear a Catholic Mass that morning. Since their union had not so far produced a healthy child of either sex, Princess Mary of Orange now found herself heir presumptive to the three thrones of England, Scotland and Ireland. Nothing suggests that she was specially ambitious for the succession but her newly exalted status had the immediate effect of improving William's already favourable relationship with the United Provinces, whatever their republican sentiments.

It also meant that a guest from England whose company William and Mary had much enjoyed would need to be moved on or else become a serious political embarrassment. Charles II's senior bastard, the Duke of Monmouth, had fetched up at The Hague in 1684, exiled from England for his rash involvement in various intrigues against the king led by disgruntled Whigs, Protestants and republicans. Many of these followed Monmouth to Holland and now encouraged him to seize his chance of claiming the throne as a champion of Protestant liberties against the threats of Catholic encroachment posed by the newly crowned King James. Though William was unwilling to offer open support for Monmouth's enterprise, he took care to warn him of a kidnap operation planned by James's agents, urging him to leave The Hague at once.

Monmouth departed for England with his supporters. The ensuing rebellion in the western counties ended in failure when his ragtag army was defeated by government forces at Sedgemoor on 6 July 1685. He himself was captured and executed and a mass hanging and transportation of rebel prisoners was ordered in the so-called 'Bloody Assizes' conducted by the sulphurous young Welsh justice Sir George Jeffreys. Though the vindictiveness of this aftermath shocked many, the actions taken gained broader approval across the nation as a whole, King James being welcomed as a more sober, hard-working and dedicated version of his pleasure-loving brother. For the time being, the implications of his devout Catholicism were overlooked by those who saw him as a safe pair of hands, essentially patriotic and a careful father to his openly Protestant daughters, Mary and Anne. With the former and her husband he corresponded regularly and the pair were dutiful in replying. Still unhappy over her marriage to a heretic, he remained hopeful that, with a little help from the Catholic envoys he sent, she might eventually surrender to the true Church.

James's obtuseness in the matter of religion affords an essential clue to his character. The narrative of those various occurrences bringing William and Mary to the English throne in 1689 tends to contradict that view of history which sedulously excludes the force of personal motivation as a contributory factor to the outcome of a specific series of events. This reign of scarcely more than three years, one of English monarchy's briefest, is notable for the thoroughness with which the king managed to squander the bankable asset of his subjects' goodwill, antagonizing whole echelons formerly dependable for their support. In his slowness of intellect, James presented a marked contrast with his quick-witted brother. An obstinate belief that he might indeed be the destined agent of England's return to Catholicism could have been forgiven him had he not tried to bring this about through the ham-fisted enforcement of an absolute authority which seemed to place him above the law. To the older generation it was a disagreeable reminder of the very same arbitrary power with which his father, King Charles I, had formerly attempted to browbeat Parliament into acknowledging his unquestioned rights as sovereign.

The worst of examples to King James was furnished by

his cousin Louis XIV. There was a genuine fear that the English monarch, if not actually summoning French arms to his assistance, would form his style on the kind of despotism being exercised across the Channel. In October 1685, Louis, having ramped up his harassment of the Huguenots, revoked the Edict of Nantes, the guarantee of religious liberty which his grandfather Henri IV had given them almost ninety years previously. French Protestants were now formally outlawed and a massive diaspora began, with many of them fleeing to England, bringing those technical skills which a sober work ethic had encouraged them to perfect in everything from textile-weaving and furniture design to engineering, metal-working and the making of optical and musical instruments.

Though James privately commended Louis for purging his kingdom of heresy, it suited his present purposes to allow the Huguenots a refuge in England. Many of their English sympathizers, however, could only view the French persecution as a harbinger of similar oppression about to be inflicted on their own nation, for the past hundred years a bulwark of Protestantism. The centenary of the Spanish Armada's defeat in 1588 was drawing near, an anniversary assuming grim significance as James started openly rewarding English Catholics with the public offices from which they had been barred during the previous reign.

Fears that popery would be imposed by force were exacerbated by the king's failure to disband his army following the suppression of Monmouth's revolt. Popular disquiet was further increased by a weasel-worded 'Declaration of Indulgence', with its ostensible purpose of abolishing the penal laws against those not conforming to the Church of England. Members of Protestant dissenting churches welcomed the Declaration, as of course did the Catholics for whose advantage it was in fact promulgated, but the document succeeded in alienating that very same Tory constituency which had once rejoiced in James's accession. Further resentment gathered as he appointed Catholics to senior positions in the armed forces and 'intruded' priests into college fellowships at Oxford and Cambridge, creating a cause célèbre when, at Magdalen College, Oxford, the fellows were summarily ejected for refusing to accept a papist president. Mary of Orange ostentatiously contributed £200 to a fund for their support.

Protestants of all persuasions were scandalized when James became the first English monarch since the Reformation to send an embassy to the pope. Ironically, the pontiff in question, Innocent XI, was keen to distance himself as quickly as possible from any such initiative. Bitterly hostile to Louis XIV and engaged in building an anti-French alliance with the help of funds from Dutch bankers, he was less moved by James's piety than wary of his diplomatic motives. When the English ambassador to the Vatican, Lord Castlemaine (cuckolded husband of Charles II's most notorious mistress), suggested to the papal foreign secretary, Cardinal Cybo, that if Innocent was prepared to make peace with Louis the pair of them could join England in attacking the United Provinces, Cybo was immediately ordered to pass the information to the Dutch through a network of Austrian and German intelligence contacts.

William would not have been especially surprised. Recent

French attempts to kidnap him had been foiled but he was alert to less open threats created in the Netherlands by James's Catholic envoys. In a typically plodding letter to Mary, the king had tried to draw her towards a more benign view of Rome and its claims of universal Christian authority. In a few years, the scope of her serious reading had greatly increased and this, combined with innate good sense and strength of purpose, allowed her methodically to rebut his arguments without forsaking her role as dutiful daughter. She politely declined to receive the Jesuit priest he sent over as intellectual reinforcement, equipped with volumes of sound doctrine.

By the beginning of 1687, it had swiftly become clear to William and Mary that a position as passive observers of events in England was no longer tenable. Demands from disaffected elements within the nation itself for some sort of intervention by William increased as James's absolutist manoeuvres grew more blatant. The prince, dedicated to what his English clerical adviser Gilbert Burnet called the 'depression of France',[5] had already grasped the potential value of the island kingdom, with its growing commercial prosperity and strengthened navy, as a counterbalance to French overlordship of continental Europe. James's drive to Catholicize his subjects, as if to follow Louis's example in dealing with the Huguenots, threatened not only to undermine this crucial strategic advantage but to provoke another civil war, with a return to the republicanism of the 1650s. France, reasoned William, must profit from an anti-Dutch alliance with whichever side triumphed in such a conflict. Subsidies from Versailles were not shoring up the English monarchy quite as sturdily as they had done for Charles II but there was an obvious danger of James ending, like his brother, as a client of their far more powerful cousin.

'If the nations of England and Scotland come once into extreme suffering that their case require it, the Prince must either hazard himself for them and become their deliverer or else he will risk and hazard his interest in these kingdoms for ever.'[6] The verdict of Patrick Hume, a Scottish Protestant refugee in the Netherlands, was widely shared in Britain and among his fellow exiles. Such motives as were available to William for invading England, should the need arise, were not confined to politics and religion. His wife's Stuart inheritance was being endangered by her father's wilful failure to comprehend the profoundly nationalistic element of defensive solidarity underpinning British Protestantism. Through her, as through his mother, William could conscientiously echo Shakespeare's Fortinbras:

> I have some rights of memory in this kingdom,
> Which now to claim my vantage doth invite me.[7]

In December 1687, the announcement that James's queen, Mary Beatrice, was pregnant posed a still more direct challenge to Mary of Orange's succession to the English throne. If the birth occurred without mishap, James was free to designate his Catholic child, born of a genuine princess as opposed to a mere lady-in-waiting, as heir, setting the semi-royal heretic half-sister aside for good. Even worse, the baby might be a boy. In view of her stepmother's earlier gynaecological problems and a rumour that her father might be impotent as a result of venereal disease, Mary remained resolutely sceptical as to the contents of 'the Queen's great belly'.[8] In this she was supported by her sister Anne, with as much to lose as she from this 'supposititious child',[9] who kept her fully informed, by letters from London, of the royal pregnancy in its various phases. To both women it looked increasingly as if the king and queen were contriving, through a deliberate falsehood, to cut them out of the royal line altogether. The realization of this proved genuinely disturbing to Mary, whose sense of the need for reciprocal loyalty between father and daughter was still strong.

For William the queen's fertility provided the tipping point for a scheme he had been contemplating, however vaguely, since his father-in-law's accession two years earlier. Throughout this period, visitors to The Hague had sought his ear as to the possibility of an invasion in which, as a commander of Protestant legions, he could set the kingdom to rights, halting the Catholic purges and guaranteeing his wife's succession. For a time he merely listened attentively. Cultivating the art of careful listening was part of an unquenchably analytical approach summed up in William Temple's comment that 'he has a way of falling downright into the bottom of a business'.[10] The prince was reluctant, nevertheless, to involve himself in a direct bid, *à la* Monmouth, to topple James, whether through a respect for the king's sovereign legitimacy or simply because, at this stage, the indicators of likely support for any such enterprise were insufficiently reliable.

By the spring of 1688, however, demands for intervention were coming not just from exiles and refugees, but from highly placed figures within the British political elite. In April, two admirals of the fleet, Edward Russell and Arthur Herbert, finally gained William's assurance that 'if he was invited by some men of the best interest ... to come and rescue the nation and the religion, he believed he could be ready by the end of September'.[11] On 10 June, Queen Mary Beatrice gave birth to a son, James Edward, forthwith proclaimed Prince of Wales, whose parentage and origins almost as instantly became topics for scurrilous gossip. Had the original baby died soon after being born? Was another male infant then smuggled into the royal apartments inside a warming pan? Why were there no Protestants present during the royal labour, but only a numerous company of Catholic grandees, priests and popish midwives? At The Hague, William and Mary of Orange duly ordered prayers to be said for the newborn heir in their private chapel. It was now that Gilbert Burnet recalled a conversation with the princess two years earlier as to her likely reaction were the queen to give birth to a son. Perhaps somewhat disingenuously, she answered that 'she was sure it would give her no concern at all on her own account'.[12]

On the present occasion, as it happened, she had taken care to send her sister Anne a detailed questionnaire, listing such items as 'Whether the milk, that, as is said, was in the Queen's breasts, was seen by many, or conducted in a mystery?', 'Who was in the room, both men and women? What time they came in and how near they stood?', 'Who is about the child, rockers and dry-nurse?' Anne's painstaking responses concluded glumly enough: 'I shall never now be satisfied, whether the child be true or false. It may be it is our brother, but God only knows . . . I shall ever be of the number of unbelievers.'[13]

Jubilation at the prince's birth was largely confined to Catholics and a small number of municipal corporations whose officials owed their positions to royal gerrymandering. The event was, in any case, thoroughly upstaged by the release, following their detention and trial, of seven Anglican bishops, led by the Archbishop of Canterbury, who had petitioned the crown to be absolved from reading the Declaration of Indulgence to their clergy and had questioned James's right of exercising his so-called 'dispensing power' to overrule the decrees of Parliament. The fact that the prelates involved had all been noted, hitherto, for their conservative acquiescence to royal policy made their arrest more offensive to a whole constituency of bien-pensant Tory Anglicans instinctively loyal to the crown.

The seven bishops' release, celebrated by bonfires, bell-ringing and the broaching of beer barrels across the nation, was a propaganda disaster for the king. It gave the cue to another group of seven, a dissident collection of leading Protestants headed by Thomas Osborne, Earl of Danby, and Henry Compton, Bishop of London, to send a letter to William urging immediate action, before James could take still more drastic measures and plunge his three kingdoms into another civil war. For these 'Immortal Seven', as they were later known, as for William and Mary themselves, an additional menace was the outright republicanism espoused by radical elements among Dissenters, malcontent Whigs and those who had rejoiced in the Cromwellian Protectorate and the Puritan 'rule of the saints' thirty years previously. Though the Prince and Princess of Orange had wide experience of conciliating the republicans of the United Provinces, neither of them was likely to countenance a similar political settlement in England and its adjacent realms.

The letter from the Immortal Seven, based on its signatories' reading of a broader national mood, as opposed to merely voicing the dissatisfaction of a privileged minority, was the starting signal William needed. During the summer of 1688, he oversaw the preparation of a massive fleet of 49 battleships and 250 transport vessels, crewed by 10,000 sailors. While Dutch land forces, together with brigades recruited among English and Scottish exiles, made ready to leave for England, his envoys in the German states allied against France were busy hiring regiments to step in to defend the Netherlands.

Even if absolute secrecy in mounting such a huge operation was impossible, it was easy to bamboozle France into believing, until too late, that this military build-up was designed to counter Louis XIV's newest campaign in the Rhine valley. William also took care to pacify Denmark, currently in dispute with the Dutch over territorial claims on the North Sea coast, while simultaneously hinting to foreign diplomats that the enlarged fleet might soon be on battle stations for a war with Danish squadrons in the Baltic. His true intentions – some of them, at least – were set before the deputies of his own United Provinces, justifying his grand strategy by convincing them of their potential danger from a King of England strengthened by the presence of his own 'hopeful prince' as Catholic heir and nursing a hatred of the Dutch which had lingered from his days as an admiral in the wars with

Holland. Nothing could now prevent James II, it seemed, from drawing closer to Louis in a wholesale crusade against Protestantism. Presentation of this doom-laden scenario marked the culmination of William's confidence-building encounters, over ten years, with the deputies, who now offered their undivided support. He still needed to clinch the issue of justification for the enterprise with an official mani-festo, couched in a style gratifying both to his natural adherents among the Whig party in England and to the grow-ing number of Tory Anglicans who viewed his armed intervention as an ultimate safeguard against popery.

William and Mary had grown to maturity in an age when the printed word was being turned to account in the cause of propaganda as never before. Their particular compact with those they eventually came to rule depended on the professional talents of a host of journalists, pamphleteers, satirists, ballad makers and authors of 'authentic reports', 'brief accounts' and 'true relations'. Wars were not confined to the smoke and stench of an actual battlefield but were fought with ink and paper in the form of polemics, apolo-gies, lampoons and caricatures by the doughty scribblers of either side. Thus William's 'Declaration of the Reasons Inducing Him to Appear in Arms in the Kingdom of Eng-land', based on a draft version by Lord Danby, mingled punch with persuasiveness, blaming everything on King James's evil advisers rather than bad-mouthing the sover-eign himself. These men were responsible, apparently, for arbitrary government, for subverting the religion, laws and liberties of the three kingdoms, for purging the judicial bench, the armed forces and the municipal corporations and for turning out the fellows of Magdalen College. The manifesto also took care to rubbish little Prince James Edward's legitimacy (genetic testing of his descendants has recently validated his Stuart parentage) and assured its readers that all these grievances would soon be redressed by a freely elected parliament.

In so far as they exerted any influence on King James, his counsellors, heedless of the growing danger, initially persuaded him to ignore the preparations afoot in Holland. By September 1688, however, French intelligence sources managed to convince him that the naval and military muster was indeed designed for a landing in England, yet even then he was sufficiently confident that a Dutch strike on the east coast – the most obvious destination – could be seen off by a fleet stationed in the Thames estuary. The season, in any case, was on his side to prevent a smooth crossing of the stormy North Sea, but he took the precaution of reinforcing shoreline defences and recruiting extra regiments for the army. Other troops were recalled from Ireland, where the high-handed measures of his Catholic viceroy, Lord Tyrconnell, had severely alienated the Protestant landholding gentry and aristocracy.

A sound of stable doors being frantically locked behind bolting horses grew louder when James began backtracking on the more extreme measures through which he had asserted his sovereign authority. The Magdalen fellows were reinstated, corporations given back their confiscated charters, ejected judges restored to the bench and the Anglican bishops conciliated with a promise that 'things past should be buried in perpetual oblivion'.[14] By now, William's Declaration was being given its final tweak and the expeditionary force stood more or less complete, its supplies including 10,000 pairs of boots, 2,000 saddles, 1,600 hogsheads of beer and 4 tons of tobacco. James's last letter to Mary is an essay in moral blackmail:

> I easily believe you may be embarrassed how to write to me, now that the unjust design of the Prince of Orange's invading me is so public. And though I know you are a good wife, and ought to be so, yet for the same reason I must believe you will be still as good a daughter to a father that has always loved you so tenderly.

Such tenderness was alloyed with menace in the closing sentence, 'You shall find me kind to you, if you desire it.'[15] The painful choice Mary now faced added a further layer of complexity to what was fast becoming one of the English monarchy's most dramatic episodes. On 26 October, William took a formal farewell of the United Provinces, telling the deputies, 'What God intends for me I do not know, but if I should fall, have a care for my beloved wife, who loves your country as her own.'[16] His audience wept and he himself was on the edge of tears. Alone with Mary, he broke down entirely, overmastered by that emotional intensity he tried so hard on other occasions to subdue. Nerving himself to begin, with the words 'If it be God's will that we should not meet once more . . .', he tailed off into silence, then told her that she should marry again. 'It was as if my heart had been pierced through,' wrote Mary in her journal:

> He himself could not pronounce these words without shedding tears and throughout the interview he showed me all the

tenderness I could desire, so much, indeed, that I shall never in my life forget it. My distress confused me but I assured him that I could never love anybody else, for assuredly I could never find his like. He answered me with so much tenderness as to increase my love for him, if that were possible.[17]

What needs to be understood about the closeness of William and Mary's relationship, as it had evolved over the past ten years (with Squinting Betty always in the middle distance), is the mutual fervour of their Protestant convictions. Speaking of the need for his wife to remarry should he meet his death in the coming venture, William added the injunction 'As you need no reminding, it must not be to a Papist',[18] then told her it was a concern for their faith which made him speak thus. There is an agreeable irony, therefore, in the fact that, when the expedition eventually set out, the Viceroy of the Spanish Netherlands (modern Belgium) ordered Masses in the churches of Catholic Brussels to be said for its success and that in Rome itself Pope Innocent XI, delighted by its triumphant progress, exclaimed: 'Salvation through our enemies!'[19] Their shared loathing of Louis XIV trumped Catholic solidarity in this crucial instance.

The whole enormous operation very nearly foundered altogether. On 30 October, the fleet set sail from Helvoetsluys but was driven back to port by ferocious gales the following day. 'You could hear the men groan after a pitiful manner'[20] as ships scattered across the North Sea and over a thousand cavalry horses died of suffocation in their holds. William's pertinacity inspired a second attempt, depending as it had to on a change in the wind. Promising Mary not to set sail without seeing her, he arranged a hasty final rendezvous at the town of Brielle. 'When he left me,' wrote Mary, 'it was as if my heart had been torn from my body . . . I stayed without moving in the room where he had left me; all that I could do was to commend him to God.'[21] On 9 November, the wind at last blew from the east and the great 600-ship flotilla embarked once more.

Sailing northwards, they seemed to be playing into the hands of King James's English navy awaiting them off the Essex shore. Suddenly, at a prearranged signal, they turned south, with 'the Protestant wind', as it became known, carrying them unmolested through the Strait of Dover and on down the Channel. Very nearly overshooting their intended landing in Torbay, with English battleships at Plymouth poised to attack, they were favoured once again by the weather. The wind dropped and a southerly breeze wafted them into the bay at sunset on 10 November. William had beguiled the tedium of the voyage by arguing with Gilbert Burnet over the Calvinist doctrine ordaining that certain elect individuals are predestined to salvation. After they came ashore at the fishing port of Brixham, the prince, according to Burnet, 'asked me, if I would not now believe [in] predestination'.[22]

Almost a month earlier, on 14 October, King James II had celebrated his fifty-fifth birthday in markedly muted fashion. The notes made that day by the diarist John Evelyn speak volumes, in their brevity, as to the mingled hope, anticipation, dread and sheer amazement gripping the nation:

14*th*. The King's Birthday. No guns from the Tower as usual. The sun eclipsed at its rising. This day signal for the victory of William the Conqueror against Harold, near Battel, in Sussex. The wind, which had been hitherto west, was east all this day. Wonderful expectation of the Dutch fleet. Public prayers ordered to be read in the churches against invasion.[23]

When, a month later, the invasion finally happened, it was not the Norman Conquest, nor even the Spanish Armada, all over again. It was like nothing anyone could remember, from English history or that of any other nation. William and Mary, at the epicentre of the crisis, had as much to learn from what took place as the humblest among those who would soon become their subjects.

3
Monarchy by Contract

What occurred next was breathtaking both in its essential outlines and the incisive suddenness with which these emerged. Harold Macmillan's apocryphal encapsulation of devastating changes in the political landscape as 'Events, dear boy, events' was never better exemplified than by the winter of 1688–9. Revisionist attempts at reducing the episode known as the Glorious Revolution to a little local difficulty stage-managed by an elite committee of fractious aristocrats and careerist clergymen are simply not borne out by evidence. The experience of change, of a profound shift, for better or worse, in the life of the nation, its structures and compacts, was universal, not limited to a single echelon but shared among people of all classes, regardless of status or influence.

The term 'revolution' was current from the outset. 'Glorious' got tacked on afterwards by Whig propagandists, the glory enhanced by a tradition that no blood was shed in the process. This is not strictly true – sporadic violence broke out across the kingdom in confrontations between supporters of William and James – but a full-scale civil war, feared by many on either side, failed to materialize. The Prince of Orange and his Dutch, English and Scottish regiments landed in Torbay on 5 November 1688 and marched north-east to Exeter, picking up support en route. Key garrisons at Plymouth and Bristol declared for the prince, and several high-ranking army officers, including Viscount Churchill, the future Duke of Marlborough, deserted King James at Salisbury to ride west and join William. As further uprisings in his favour were orchestrated by local magnates in Yorkshire, the Midlands and East Anglia, James watched his sovereignty disintegrate. After a botched attempt at negotiating with his son-in-law, he fled to France, the protection of Louis XIV and a penurious exile at the chateau of Saint-Germain-en-Laye, outside Paris, amid his loyal Catholic entourage.

The Prince of Orange arrived in London at the head of his invasion force on the rain-swept afternoon of 18 December. Vast, jubilant crowds braving the weather to welcome him were not rewarded with much in the way of engaging smiles, graceful bows or a wave of the princely hand. Many of William's newfound English adherents were becoming unnerved by the resonant profundity of his hermetic silences. He might have reminded some of them of Duke Vincentio in Shakespeare's *Measure for Measure*, who declares:

> . . . I love the people,
> But do not like to stage me to their eyes;
> Though it do well, I do not relish well
> Their loud applause and Aves vehement;
> Nor do I think the man of safe discretion
> That does affect it.[1]

Mary, trying too hard to make up for her husband's coldness with a charm offensive, earned criticism for her 'strange and unbecoming' conduct.[2] John Evelyn noted that 'she came into Whitehall laughing and jolly, as to a wedding, so as to seem quite transported ... This carriage was censured by many.'[3]

After all, William was not yet a king, of England or anywhere else, and at this critical juncture of his fortunes it wasn't necessarily certain that he would become one, given the terms offered him by the interim government, styled the Convention, which the House of Lords had hastily scrambled together. While his control of public order in the capital and throughout the kingdom might be a fait accompli, he was unwilling to accept either the role of prince consort to Mary, crowned as queen in her own right, or (worse where he was concerned) the regency of a realm still under nominal rule by his uncle, whom a group of peers and bishops proposed recalling from France. Lord Halifax, a major operator in the political settlement now being hammered out, gracelessly put it to William: 'You may be what you please. As nobody knows what to do with you, so nobody knows what to do without you.'[4]

To such an anomalous position, unprecedented in the history of European, let alone English monarchy, we owe a key element in the governmental structure of modern Britain, the limited functionality of the sovereign in relation to that of Parliament. The speedy evolution of this new arrangement during the thirteen-year reign which followed owes much to William's consistency, his firmness of purpose and his realistic willingness to embrace compromise or accept failure where giving ground might ultimately help towards fulfilling his wider personal ambitions. As for Mary, her role in the 1689 settlement was crucial to the terms finally agreed upon. She had already resolved not to accept the crown without William beside her. 'I am the prince's wife,' she told Lord Danby, 'and would never be other than what I should be in conjunction with him ... I shall take it extremely unkindly if any, under pretence of their care for me, should set up a divided interest between me and the prince.'[5] Summoned by a letter from William, she embarked for England on 8 February 1689 and in April the pair were jointly crowned in Westminster Abbey, with what the new king, with a Calvinist shudder, called 'quaint old Popish ceremonies'.[6] The Archbishop of Canterbury having refused, on grounds of loyalist conscience, to conduct the coronation service, it was performed instead by Henry Compton, Bishop of London, one of the Immortal Seven.

'The hand of God has advanced me to the crown,' wrote William to his aunt Albertine, 'I hope it will be to His Glory, but it is no small burden that I have to carry.'[7] To her journal Mary confided: 'My heart is not made for a kingdom.'[8] Whatever their misgivings, the pair, by becoming King William III and Queen Mary II, joint sovereigns of England, had achieved a unique status in the annals of world monarchy. This anomalous phenomenon – as if some sort of weird royal hermaphrodite had been spawned – explains the widespread distribution among their subjects of its dual image. The couple's fate was to become a celebrity icon, their crowned likenesses adorning everything from earthenware dishes, fans and playing cards to banners, song sheets and medals.

If we discount the botched attempt by the Dudleys and Seymours in 1554 to make a puppet queen out of their kinswoman, the hapless Lady Jane Grey, William and Mary are England's only example of monarchy as product or construct. Each of them had a share in fashioning it. For all the hysterical Jacobite denunciations of Mary as a parricide (her father was still very much alive) and William as a usurper (James having left his throne in the lurch when he could easily have confronted his son-in-law) there had been no murder or use of violence shadowing their progress to the throne. The notion of English kingship as embodying a contractual bond between the sovereign and the people, an idea which had assumed looming significance during the Civil War era, was now reformulated so as to enable continuity within the framework of civil society and national governance. To this extent the Glorious Revolution was conservative, in that the established hierarchy was not overturned and state institutions, crown, Church and Parliament, were preserved intact.

What changed for ever was the accepted understanding of a monarch's role in the life of the kingdom. That 'divinity [which] doth hedge a king'[9] had substantially diminished by the time those quaint old popish ceremonies placed the crowns on the two royal heads. The Convention parliament had resolved '[t]hat King James the Second, having endeavoured to subvert the Constitution of the Kingdom, by breaking the original Contract between King and People . . . has abdicated the Government'. In addition, it concluded '[t]hat it hath been found, by experience, to be inconsistent with the safety and welfare of this Protestant Kingdom, to be governed by a Popish Prince'.[10] That phrase 'by experience' is vital to our understanding of the contemporary mood in an England where scientific enquiry and the life of the mind had flourished so freely and abundantly throughout the century. It emphasizes the fundamental dividing line between Catholic and Protestant, between dogma imparted through received wisdom or ecclesiastical authority and truths established in a climate of 'experimental philosophy' and unfettered intellectual curiosity.

The newfangled monarchical template was not all about religion. Prudently, if at the same time reluctantly, William and Mary accepted the terms – or at any rate the essence – of a Declaration of Rights drawn up by House of Commons committees and amended by the Lords. This brought together an appeal to ancient privileges enjoyed by Parliament and by ordinary subjects, an attack on the royal dispensing power so notoriously exercised by King James and an implicit vindication of Parliament's centrality to the business of government, requiring its frequent sessions. By the time this passed into statute as the Bill of Rights on 16 December 1689, the concept of English monarchy had been effectively transformed into an office defined as one of public duty and fiduciary responsibility. The fact that the Declaration of Rights was read out at the coronation, before the actual moment of crowning, had its own admonitory resonance. What William and Mary thus acknowledged was not a total surrender of their power and influence but the genesis of a realm in which royal prerogative was more severely limited than ever before, popular consent was fundamental and the line of succession to the throne was determined by an adherence to Protestant principles.

A religious Toleration Act, passed in 1689, provided one of the earliest tests for the effectiveness of this new dispensation. Baffled by hardline Tories and conservative Anglican clergy in an early effort of his to secure abolition of laws excluding Protestant Dissenters and Roman Catholics from public office, William nevertheless persisted with an attempt to guarantee them greater freedom of worship. Though his continued pressure succeeded in carrying the Toleration Act through Parliament and on to the statute book, further obstructive manoeuvres from the same quarter meant that its provisions were limited to Dissenters alone. Ideally, raised in a multi-faith society, he would have preferred to see penal constraints lifted from papists as well. His closest friends included the devoutly Catholic prince and princesse de Vaudémont and his European alliance against France depended on Catholic support from Austria and Savoy, not to speak of encouragement, as noted earlier, from Rome itself. William, whatever his ingrained Calvinist distaste for popery, was never a bigot or disposed to persecute those of other confessions. Though the Toleration Act was thus essentially a fudge, it was also a contributory element towards that evolution of an enlightened civil society which defines William and Mary's reign. 'Not perhaps so wide in scope as might be wished for,' was philosopher John Locke's verdict on the legislation. 'Still, it is something to have progressed so far.'[11]

Learning to negotiate the zigzags of English politics was

no less problematic for William than coping with the beastly weather and a smog-polluted London which played havoc with his asthma. The habitual cleanliness of The Hague, always surprising to foreign visitors, contrasted powerfully with the filth and stench amid which the English chose to live. The new king had little taste for the court culture inherited from life at the Palace of Whitehall under his father-in-law and uncle, with its lechery, gambling and gossip. Unlike Mary, he was not especially fond of music and parties and there was little time to indulge the passion for hunting and hard riding with which he had exorcised the cares of state in the Netherlands. Obsessed with a need to set England's public affairs to rights and more than ever dedicated to hard work, William began to acquire the character of a charmless loner – 'a devious, dour, asthmatic, weedy foreigner' in one modern historian's phrase[12] – which has dogged him ever since. Known to very few was the inner William, adored by Mary, loved by Bentinck and Keppel, admired by Temple and Burnet, engaging, interested, funny, perceptive, straight-talking and loyal.

On Mary, prizing these qualities in him, rested almost the entire burden of public relations on the couple's behalf as king and queen. Her position as James's daughter, occupying the throne of her living father, made her vulnerable to criticism even from those who had welcomed the Revolution in principle. The cri de cœur 'My heart is not made for a kingdom', quoted earlier, was wholly sincere and there was little for her to enjoy in the suddenly exalted role of England's queen: 'I found my self here very much neglected, lit[t]le respected, censured by all, commended by none.'[13] Like her husband, she quickly learned that hardly any of the English nobility and gentry surrounding her could be regarded as completely trustworthy and that their wives and daughters, in the capacity of ladies-in-waiting and bedchamber women, were equally disingenuous in their parade of confidentiality. Like them she gave a performance: as the gracious sovereign going to the play; walking in the park; attending charity fairs; overseeing plans for new churches; or listening to the flattery of the hack poets supplying her annual birthday odes, set to music with such sparkling fancy and sumptuousness by Henry Purcell. Unlike most of her court, though, Mary was not hard-nosed enough to develop an adequate armour of cynicism and insincerity, yet, however vulnerable and insecure, she gave the day-to-day business of jobbing royalty her best shot. The effort cost her dear and would help to kill her.

Her task was made no easier when, in the summer of 1690, she found herself left in charge of domestic affairs. William had set out for Ireland to take over from the elderly German field marshal Frederick Schomberg (formerly in Louis XIV's service until exiled as a Protestant) as commander of the army fighting the forces of King James. The previous year England, with its allies Austria, Spain and Brandenburg, had declared war on France. Under Louis's auspices, the Irish expedition was the deposed monarch's first major attempt to recover his errant kingdoms. At first the Irish war followed a somewhat desultory course, with James failing to demonstrate adequate generalship and organization of his troops, and the opposing army, under

Schomberg, making an insufficient impact by its marches and countermarches.

William, now in charge, was never quite as good a tactician as he reckoned himself and lost most of the battles he fought. His ultimate victory over Louis, in what became known as the Nine Years War, would be achieved through a mixture of extraordinary personal courage, attention to detail, commitment to the task in hand and leadership from the front. The 37,000-strong army he now commanded was a polyglot force composed of English, Scottish and northern Irish regiments alongside his crack Dutch infantry brigades, French Huguenot legions and units from Denmark and Prussia. His realistic objective was to knock James out of the war so that he himself could concentrate on the more important confrontation with Louis's forces on the European stage: 'It is absolutely necessary that I try to put an end to this affair before I can think of another.'[14] The presence of an Anglo-Dutch naval squadron off the Irish coast acted as a temporary reinforcement against further troop movements from France.

The armies, Williamite and Jacobite, confronted each other west of Drogheda (a town with its own grim resonance in recent Irish history) beside the River Boyne on 1 July 1690. The previous day, while dining in full view of the Jacobite gunners, William was hit on the right shoulder by a cannon shot, 'as to take away his outward coat, shamway [chamois] wastcoat, shirt and all, and to draw near half a spoonfull of blood'.[15] 'That came near enough,' he said in Dutch, before switching to French with a curt demand to his officers: 'Messieurs, pourquoi ne marchez-vous pas?'[16] The wound was hastily patched up and the king mounted his horse, but everybody in either army would soon perceive just how crucial to victory his survival had been. Essentially the forthcoming battle was about William of Orange. The size of each army (the Jacobites numbered some thirty thousand, not significantly fewer) mattered far less than the visible presence in the field of the little hook-nosed rider who represented, according to taste, either a heroic deliverer or a scoundrelly usurper.

It was William's continuing presence at the heart of the action which decided the day. Though the Jacobite cavalry, led by James's best Irish general, Patrick Sarsfield, acquitted itself with signal bravery, the infantry was easily outgunned by the new flintlock muskets in the hands of the Dutch and Huguenot regiments. Modern historians with anti-William animus seem to imply something unsporting in the possession of this state-of-the-art weapon, as though to strip the victors of as much glory as possible by suggesting that their triumph was merely a technological fluke. Despite all their efforts at discrediting the king, what cannot be denied is his bravery in the field. His wound from the cannon shot disabled his sword arm, so he rode into battle brandishing a walking stick in his left hand and had to dispense with the customary metal cuirass as protection for his upper body. Undaunted, he saw it as his duty to lead by example. '[T]he businesse of this day had often stopt if his Majesties vigour had not pushed all forward,' wrote the King's private secretary, Sir Robert Southwell.[17]

James, on the other hand, quickly disheartened by the course of the battle, earned contempt from both his Irish and French troops for the speed with which he hastened back to Dublin. 'Séamas an Chaca', or 'James the Turd', was a name sticking all too easily after his precipitate flight to France, which he later blamed on his generals' bad advice. William's failure to follow up the Boyne victory has been criticized from both sides but was based on a realistic assessment of Jacobite strategy and news of a French fleet off Ireland's south coast. After an abortive attempt at seizing the stronghold of Limerick, thwarted by a resourceful Patrick Sarsfield, the king returned to England, confident by now that the Boyne had effectively ended serious Jacobite resistance. Armed conflict in Ireland, however, dragged on for another year until the Battle of Aughrim, in July 1691, brought hostilities to a blood-soaked close. William's attempt at securing just and moderate surrender terms for combatant Catholics would be frustrated by a Protestant parliament in Dublin. Irish historians prefer to emphasize instead his generous reward of forfeited estates to Bentinck, Keppel and Elizabeth Villiers. Whether as the sainted Protestant liberator on Orange lodge banners in the Six Counties' marching season or as the cynical opportunist giving away slices of Meath and Roscommon to his bed-fellows, William's achievement in Ireland has been squashed out of recognizable shape by ensuing centuries of grudge and grievance on either side.

But how exactly was this campaign, let alone those awaiting him in continental Europe, to be paid for? William's resolve that England should finance his 'depression of France' was inflexible and, for the first eight years of his reign, every address he made to Parliament reiterated a demand for money to fight the ongoing war between the alliance and King Louis's armies. It is perhaps less astonishing that the Lords and Commons should have assented to these continued requests if we remember how potent was the general fear of a French invasion, threatening to impose popery and destroy English rights and liberties. Though it was another fifty years before Thomas Arne and James Thomson produced their show-stopping 'Rule, Britannia!', the notion of the freeborn Englishman, of those Britons who 'never, never, never shall be slaves', was already gaining ground, as loyal propagandists fostered the concept of a nation at war for its soul under William's leadership. For all their incidental grumbling, his subjects were generally acquiescent in the raising of new revenues created by a land tax, enlarged customs duties and levies on everything from salt, funerals and hackney carriages (ancestors of today's taxicabs) to malt, hops and the beer made from them.

To service the monarch's operational needs in Europe a financial revolution began unrolling, set in motion by the fiscal dexterity of politicians and crown servants responsive to royal demands but also harnessing the City of London's mercantile enterprise and the individual talents of outstanding figures in the intellectual life of the age. Scientist Isaac Newton became Master of the Mint, philosopher John Locke turned economic theorist with his treatises on the deregulation of interest rates, and statistician Gregory King studied the earning potential among different social classes. In 1693 the concept of a national debt was launched with a Treasury loan secured by a 14 per cent annuity and a lottery with prizes funded from newly imposed taxation.

The following year saw this system of 'Publick Credit' guaranteed by a national Bank of England, a chartered corporation whose notes of exchange soon became a standard form of payment in transactions of every kind. The City, whose merchants had largely endorsed the Revolution settlement, now became the centre of a new culture of financial risk, venture and speculation, where 'stockjobbers' traded market tips in the coffee houses, while insurance companies, another novelty of the age, took premiums on housing and life expectancy. Meanwhile, the administrative machinery of government grew exponentially, with the establishment of a Customs Inspectorate, a parliamentary Public Accounts Committee scrutinizing state expenditure, and a Board of Trade, instituted by William himself in 1696 to oversee commercial activity in England's American and Caribbean colonies.

During the king's long periods of absence abroad, the hands-on business of ruling the three kingdoms became the duty of a distinctly reluctant Mary. 'I found myself now at Whitehall as in a new world,' she told her journal, 'deprived of all that was dear to me in the person of my husband, left alone among those that were perfect strangers to me . . . the great Council of a strange composition, the Cabinet Council not much better.'[18] For two people who set such a premium on trust and loyalty, their ministers were a generally slippery collection, sized up with a ruthless precision in Mary's notes to William. The Duke of Devonshire appeared 'weack and obstinate, made a meer tool by his party'; Lord Mordaunt was half mad; Lord Danby, though dependable, was 'of a temper I can never like'. She had some inkling that

Admiral Russell, initially reliable, had started a clandestine correspondence with the exiled King James. So had the self-serving John Churchill, Earl of Marlborough, of whom Mary pronounced ominously: 'I will say nothing, because it is he I could say the most of and will never trust or esteem.'[19]

The queen evidently surprised and impressed the Cabinet council with her shrewdness and practicality, her willingness to listen and her grasp of detail. They were allowed to know nothing of her fundamental insecurity, her migraines and bouts of depression, exacerbated by the growing difference with her sister, Princess Anne, over the latter's obsessive dependence on Marlborough's domineering wife, Sarah, her Lady of the Bedchamber. Mutual dislike between William and Anne was turned into serious antipathy through Sarah's manipulative bullying of her mistress in everything from demanding an increased Civil List allowance, being given tenancy of Richmond Palace and obtaining a senior army staff post for Anne's oafish husband, Prince George of Denmark. Among themselves Anne, George and the Marlboroughs turned William into a monster they nicknamed Caliban after the 'savage and deformed slave' in Shakespeare's *The Tempest*. Years later, Sarah, in this connection, recalled a private dinner at which the king, queen and princess had all been present. A dish of the season's first crop of peas was served. Anne, always a hearty eater and pregnant besides, was 'afraid to look at them, and yet could hardly keep her eyes off them'. Mary having declined her portion, William, 'without offering the Princess the least share of them, ate every one himself'.[20] This story is invariably told against the surly Dutch glutton, but another, entirely different take on it proposes William as so intensely preoccupied with cares of state that the act of wolfing the dish became one of absent-mindedness rather than selfish gourmandizing.

His chronic asthma made the rambling old palace of Whitehall, surrounded by the smoke of London, insufferable as a royal residence. Soon after arriving in England, he and Mary began seeking a healthier microclimate at Hampton Court amid its Thameside woods and fields. Here Sir Christopher Wren was commissioned to design a new range of royal apartments, built in brick with stone facings and handsomely fitted out as an enfilade of panelled rooms with frescoed ceilings, woodcarving by Grinling Gibbons and special shelves and niches for displaying Mary's collection of blue and white Chinese porcelain.

A similar arrangement characterized the couple's alterations to the house they bought from Lord Nottingham in the village of Kensington, reached along muddy highroads on either side of Hyde Park. Here Wren, Gibbons and their team of craftsmen and masons created an elegant little winter palace – 'a very sweet villa', as John Evelyn called it[21] – unpretentious from without but inside reflecting its new owners' absorption with every aspect of interior decor, from curtains and carpets to suites of dining-room furniture and theatrical state beds hung with the vibrantly colourful flower-printed Indian fabrics now being imported from Bengal by the East India Company.

This shared passion for home-making bridged the emotional divide between William and Mary, widened by Elizabeth Villiers's continuing presence at court and by the king's prolonged absences on campaign with his Dutch male entourage. While still in Holland as prince and princess, they had purchased an old manor house at Het Loo, south-east of Amsterdam, rebuilt as a royal country retreat amid extensive gardens laid out in parterres and terraces with fountains and canals. The writer Daniel Defoe, who became William's staunch admirer and loyal propagandist, credits the king with reviving a love of gardening in England through his horticultural projects at Hampton Court and Kensington. This royal influence can be seen at work in the Dutch-style gardens created for country houses across the nation during the seventeenth century's last years. A whole culture of plant nurseries, importing exotic species and developing new hybrids and varieties flourished during the period as proof of the reinvigorated enthusiasm for this pastime.

Teaching their subjects how to live comfortably and agreeably in their houses, cultivate their gardens and apply serious criteria of style to the spaces, interior or exterior, which surrounded them was an enduring and radical contribution by William and Mary to the changing nature of Englishness. In a world of rapidly increasing affluence and opportunity, this was a revolution witnessed not just by the mushrooming of superior artisan businesses to cater for such new domesticity – the cabinet maker, fringe maker, upholsterer, seedsman and plantsman – but by a greater attention (Dutch-inspired) to cleanliness and personal hygiene, together with correspondingly stricter standards of public morality and polite conduct. The dominant resonance of the 1690s is that of the English learning to behave themselves under the tutelage of their joint sovereigns – good examples, give or take a dish of new peas.

4
A Lonely Crown

Classicists, convinced that everything of value in Western culture happened in the ancient Mediterranean before the Common Era, like to remind us that we owe our democracy to the Greeks. Such a condescending view, in England at least, is entirely unjustified by the facts of the case. These are that during the course of six or seven hundred years, from the days of the Saxon kings to the reign of Queen Elizabeth, the nation evolved its own form of popular sovereignty in the shape of a parliament whose members, over the generations, were almost entirely unconscious of the glories of Periclean Athens and the age of Socrates and Plato. The words 'democracy' and 'democratic' found their way into the language as Elizabethan and Jacobean parliaments grew more confident of their powers and significance in relation to the crown. To the horrified astonishment of other states, this elected assembly would end up not only waging war on its sovereign but putting him on trial, finding him guilty of crimes against the people and sentencing him to public execution.

Far from owing anything to the Greeks, modern democratic governmental systems across the world take their origin from the compromises reached with the English parliament by King William III – so patiently and presciently, whatever his private anger or frustration – during the 1690s. As a result of this achievement, England became a state in which popular representation, however limited the franchise, acted as a bulwark against tyranny, managed the national exchequer, proposed and enacted all new legislation and formed a permanent central element within the executive. As such, its example was a crucial inspiration both to the Americans in 1775 and the French in 1789, though each would far prefer to ignore such indebtedness in favour of a founding myth of national exceptionalism.

Among English monarchs, in this sphere as in others, William is the ultimate Aunt Sally for partisan historians, a king who could never get anything right. Forsaking England in pursuit of foreign wars, he never got to know his people. He was monomaniacally absorbed with squeezing taxes out of Parliament to fund these military adventures. He dragged the nation into a theatre of European affairs from which it gained no genuine advantage and are still rueing the consequences. For the sake of all this, he cynically exploited party divisions, contributing to the political acrimony and contention clouding the reign of his sister-in-law and successor, Queen Anne. All these accusations have been flung at William and none of them is wholly deserved. The practical wisdom he shared with Mary taught him to make the best, as king, of the circumstances and human resources at his disposal. Since there was no question that either would be permitted to reign without Parliament, William very quickly learned to focus his skills on cultivating a relationship with both Houses which, if not always harmonious, could produce some sort of profitable outcome. In the presence of the assembled peers and MPs, he appeared charming and conciliatory, telling them how glad he was to meet them once more and apologizing for giving them so much work to do. '[I]t might have been more agreeable to you, in relation to your Private Concerns, not to have met again so soon,' he conceded, opening the October session of 1689; 'yet the Interest of the Public lays an indispensable Obligation upon Me to Call you together at this Time.'[1] His frank declaration, made earlier that year, that 'I must leave it to you . . . to judge what Forms may be most proper to bring those Things to pass for the Good of the Nation, which I am confident are in all your Minds' has absolutely no precedent among earlier English kings in their dealings with Parliament.[2]

Though such speeches were drafted in French – William spoke his mother's language perfectly well but it ranked third among several – before being translated for his Cabinet council, the tone and direction of each were his own. The political management of ministers and parties was a far trickier battlefield than any in his French wars. Divisions between Whig and Tory, set aside during the Revolution, hardened once more as Parliament took the governmental initiative, emboldened by William's evident need for its enabling presence. Even if the Whigs, following a revolution which seemed to vindicate most of their earlier aspirations, looked like his natural constituency, it was the Tories, 'the party he thincks alone will support the throne',[3] as Mary observed, whom William for some time tended to favour. Yet he was continuously anxious to preserve some sort of neutrality in dealing with a parliament riven with shifting loyalties and the clash of personal ambitions among its factions and splinter groups. By mixing his cabinets and making either side feel valued and significant, William used his royal authority to shape the kind of consensus which should effectively underpin the ongoing war effort in Europe. A novel kind of political culture, in essence still with us, developed correspondingly, based on management of party machinery within Parliament itself, on a greater importance accorded by members to the business of wooing their constituents for votes and on a propaganda industry of print journalism, pamphleteering and verse satire which would harness the talents of some of the age's finest writers, including Jonathan Swift, Joseph Addison, Richard Steele and Daniel Defoe.

The king was obviously happier when distant from political warfare in Westminster and Grub Street, riding instead amid the genuine smoke and carnage of battles on the plains of Flanders. To King Louis's annoyance William was rapidly gaining European fame as a military champion, loved by his troops and respected among international allies. Even if the bloody engagements at Steinkerk in 1692 and Landen the following year were officially chalked up as French victories, it was soon perceived that William's tenacity had turned each battle into a crucial holding operation, serving to deplete his enemy's resources and thus scotch the hitherto resistless northward push by Louis's army towards the Dutch frontier. In England, however, such apparent reverses for the king and his allies were misjudged, leading to the seditious suggestion by one satirist that the joint sovereigns should swap roles: 'Will should have knotted and Moll gone to Flanders.'[4]

'Knotting of fringe', whether as knitting or macramé work, was one of Mary's best-loved pastimes, a therapy keeping her grounded as she oversaw the domestic affairs of a kingdom growing disenchanted with her absent husband, 'the Dutch abortion' as Anne and the Marlboroughs freely referred to him. There was no such thing in those days as a royal diary secretary but we know enough about Mary's commitments while William was away to appreciate their staggering volume. With Sir Christopher Wren (whom the king had loyally supported when part of the new Hampton Court building collapsed) she planned a hospital for sailors in Charles II's unfinished royal palace at Greenwich and sent a personal appeal for loyalty to their potentially treacherous officers at Portsmouth, duly shamed into responding with an address which ended: 'God Almighty . . . preserve Your Majestys most Sacred Person, direct Your Councils and prosper Your Arms.'[5] She took upon herself the nomination of virtuoso preacher John Tillotson as Archbishop of Canterbury, a liberal 'latitudinarian' within the Church of England, accused by conservatives of doing more for 'the spreading and rooting of atheism than fifty Spinosa's [or] Hobbs's'[6] but during his brief tenure (1691–4) an outstanding primate.

The queen gave her blessing (and funds) to the founding of a new American university, the College of William & Mary in Virginia. She scrutinized the administration of the Treasury, the appointment of army officers and university dons and the pay claims of public employees. She also undertook a project dear to both her and William, that of the reformation of manners, with the help of laws against blasphemy, swearing and drunkenness, an initiative proving especially popular among the dissenting communities newly heartened by the Toleration Act. At her court, meanwhile, the prevailing tone contrasted notably with the moral laxity of previous reigns, influencing a general shift throughout the 1690s towards a greater sophistication and formality in the habits of English society. If Mary and William were not exactly a Victoria and Albert *avant la lettre* in this context, each saw nothing inappropriately hypocritical (since a court atmosphere tended to encourage loose morals) in trying to make their particular version of royalty dignified and respectable.

For her subjects Mary had become the public face of monarchy, growing, as Gilbert Burnet noted, 'so universally beloved that nothing could stand against her in the affections of the nation'.[7] William, as she knew all too well, was fatally indifferent to popularity. The burden of a crown was reflected in some of her private comments to friends and relations. To Rachel Russell, widow of a man Charles II had turned into a martyr for liberty by sending to the scaffold, she acknowledged that she had 'cause enough to think this life not so fine a thing as, it may be, others do'.[8] To her father's cousin, Electress Sophia of Hanover, she sounded a still more gloomy note: 'In this world each one carries his cross – mine is not light but one must submit.'[9]

Her task was made no easier by continuing strife with Anne over the latter's dependency on Sarah Churchill and by the discovery that a plot by Jacobites and French agents to assassinate King William had involved King James. '[H]e who I dare no more name father was consenting to the barbarous murder of my husband ... I fancied I should be pointed at as the daughter of one who was capable of such things.'[10] Far from alienating William, as Mary initially feared, the revelation evoked in him a brief access of solicitude and concern for his wife in what she called 'my great and endless misfortune'.[11]

Occasionally her innate sense of fun broke through to lighten the load. She teased Lord Nottingham, secretary of state and the only minister she really trusted, for being too obsessed with arresting suspected Jacobite conspirators simply to make up numbers 'as they empanel jurymen'. Entering the council chamber with Burnet at her side and surveying the assembled lords in full knowledge that most of them were in correspondence with her father and his exiled court at Saint-Germain, she shocked him by cynically quoting the prophet Ezekiel's famous question: 'Can such dry bones live?', a devastating verdict on those purporting to be her devoted servants.[12]

Pleasure for Mary came in the form of adding to her furniture and porcelain collections, buying new books for her library at Kensington and the occasional ball at which William, an excellent dancer, condescended to assist. Music was still a great solace but not always of the most sophisticated kind. One afternoon she summoned the stupendous Chapel Royal bass John Gostling and the virtuoso singer and lutenist Arabella Hunt to entertain her. Their accompanist on the harpsichord was Henry Purcell, several of whose songs they performed, until 'at length the queen beginning to grow tired, asked Mrs Hunt if she could not sing the old Scots ballad "Cold and Raw"'.[13] Mary's request for a simple folk song after an hour or so of art music is perfectly forgivable. Shortly afterwards, in that year's ode (his fourth) for her birthday, 'Love's Goddess Sure was Blind', Purcell used 'Cold and Raw' as the ground bass for an air praising her drive for moral reform: 'May her blest example chase / Vice in troops out of the land'. Was this musical allusion, as most writers on Purcell (the present author included) have assumed, the composer's sly revenge or just a nice birthday bonbon cheekily tucked inside the gorgeous intricacies of his mature style?

Under the cares of state, Mary's hitherto robust good health began to weaken. At the reign's outset it was little William, dwarfed by his strapping wife, whose pale, sickly, stunted appearance gave concern. Now Mary, putting on weight, became wracked with headaches, skin rashes and nausea. In a letter of 1694, she ruefully acknowledged that habitual worry and sorrow had destroyed her looks, bringing on middle age when she was only thirty-two years old. Would her husband still love her? A sinister omen appeared when a ruby dropped out of the ring he had given her after their wedding ceremony. Meanwhile, Elizabeth Villiers, *en poste* as her lady-in-waiting, remained squinting from the shadows at Kensington.

When William returned to England on 9 November 1694, with the war finally turning in his favour, Mary met him at Rochester and the pair were greeted en route to London by the kind of ecstatic crowds, bonfires and bell-ringing which made it seem like 1688 all over again. Once home,

William promptly retired with a fever, dosed by his wife with apples and milk, while he took copious spoonfuls of quinine, known in those days as 'Jesuits' bark', due to its use among missionary priests in the forests of Paraguay.

No such remedy availed Mary when, on 19 December, already suffering from a heavy cold, she noticed that a rash had broken out on her arms and shoulders. Recognizing this at once for a symptom of smallpox, she ordered all her servants who had not already had the disease to leave Kensington Palace at once. Through the night and into the small hours of next morning, having shut herself in her closet, she methodically sorted her private papers, burning all letters from her husband, her father and her girlhood friends, making individual bequests, including several to pauper children she had taken under her wing, and leaving instructions for the payment of her debts. Not until this process was complete did she send for William, busy at Whitehall with government despatches. She had written a special letter for him, which, though destroyed by scrupulous courtiers of a later generation, we know to have contained 'strong but decent admonition' as to his relationship with Elizabeth Villiers.[14] It appears to have charged him not only with sacrificing her happiness to the ongoing liaison but with compromising his own hopes of salvation.

Taking to her bed, Mary now permitted the doctors to examine her. William, who had arrived to assume the role of chief nurse, swooned on receiving their diagnosis, then collapsed in bitter, hysterical sobbing, refusing all attempts at consolation from the attendant clergy. 'There is no hope for the queen,' he gasped to Burnet. 'From being the happiest, I am now the miserablest creature upon earth. I have never known one single fault in her!'[15] The depth of his abject despair caused everyone present to wonder whether he might actually die before his wife. After an agonizing week, made worse on Christmas Day by a delusive moment of remission, Mary faced her end calmly, telling Thomas Tenison (Tillotson's successor as Archbishop of Canterbury) that 'she had nothing then to do, but to look up to God, and submit to his will'.[16] Considerate to the last, she invited Tenison to ignore protocol and sit down. After taking a final communion, with prayers and psalms, she experienced a brief, delirious regression to the fear, born in childhood, that her parents were trying to lure her into the Catholic fold, murmuring her suspicion that one of the doctors had 'put a popish Nurse upon me',[17] who was hiding behind a screen near her bed. Early on the morning of 28 December 1694, Queen Mary II died.

William, by now almost suicidal with grief, retreated from public view as Parliament, whose assembled members had wept on receiving news of the queen's death, took charge of her magnificent funeral, unaware, for the time being, of Mary's own wish for 'no extraordinary expense'.[18] The coffin alone cost a staggering £850, there was a grand lying-in-state at the Banqueting House in Whitehall, followed a week later by the most elaborate obsequies ever performed for an English monarch. 'Never was so universal a mourning' was how John Evelyn summed it up.[19] On a snowy March day, the cortège, with the royal body borne on a catafalque designed by Christopher Wren, was accompanied by 400 poor women in black gowns, each with a

boy train-bearer, witnesses to Mary's charity. The inter-
ment at Westminster Abbey was made memorable by
Henry Purcell's anthem 'Thou knowest, Lord, the secrets
of our hearts', accompanied by the 'flat Mournfull Trum-
pets' which had played his funeral march during the
procession.[20]

'[S]he was such an admirable woman . . . as does, if possible,
outdo the renowned Queen Elizabeth,' concluded Evelyn.[21]
Mary's death and the grandeur of the ceremonies attending it
marked an extraordinary propaganda coup for the Revolution monarchy. She had reigned, after all, for barely five years.
Though one seditious parson dared to take as his biblical text
for a commemorative sermon the words 'Go now see now this
cursed Woman and bury her, for she is a King's Daughter',[22]
the overwhelming popular reaction evinced a genuine sense of
loss and a corresponding compassion for her husband. Sorrow
was not confined to England. The Dutch mourned a
much-loved Princess of Orange but it was France where
Mary's passing made the most unexpected impact. By now,
attitudes to King James at Louis XIV's court had shifted from
generous outrage at his plight in exile to exasperated bore-
dom. 'The more one sees of this King,' said William's cousin
Liselotte, duchesse d'Orléans, 'the more favourably one feels
towards the Prince of Orange.' Madame de Sévigné was as
pitilessly succinct: 'Listening to him talk, you realize why he is
here.'[23] Thus when James forbade mourning at Saint-Germain
and persuaded Louis to do likewise at Versailles, the French
nobility ostentatiously absented itself from court functions for
a suitable season as a mark of respect for Mary and her
bereaved husband.

1. William of Orange by Adriaen Hanneman, 1654, wearing the 'long clothes' favoured for seventeenth-century male infants. Note the symbolic orange tree.

2. Princess Mary of York, from a family group portrait by Peter Lely, c.1668–85

3. William of Orange at twenty years old, already the serious young military campaigner, by Willem Wissing, *c*.1670

4. Mary as Princess of Orange by Peter Lely, 1677, capturing the charm and elegance which made her popular in the Netherlands

5. *The Protestant Grind-Stone*, a 1690 cartoon showing William and Mary pressing the pope's nose to a grindstone. In fact Pope Innocent XI was one of their most enthusiastic supporters.

6. The Battle of the Boyne by Jan Wyck, 1690, displays William typically in the thick of the combat.

7. William III posed for this remarkable likeness by Godfried Schalcken, *c.*1692–7, while holding the candle 'till the tallow ran down upon his fingers'.

8. Mary II by Godfrey Kneller, 1690. The cares of monarchy begin to take their toll of the reluctant queen's face and figure.

9. Princess Anne and William Henry, Duke of Gloucester. Fondness for the little boy reconciled his mother and King William following Mary's death.

10. Leonard Knyff's 1702 view of Hampton Court shows Christopher Wren's new buildings and the splendid formal gardens beyond.

11. An apotheosis of William and Mary is the focus of James Thornhill's ceiling in the Painted Hall of Greenwich Naval College, the queen's own foundation.

12. William III portrayed by John Bacon as a Roman general in London's St James's Square

13. William as Protestant deliverer in a modern Belfast mural

'As for this world, it is nothing to me now,' wrote William to his old friend and fellow soldier Charles-Henri de Vaudémont.[24] The tragic irony of his marriage to Mary was that she should have needed to die in order for him to reveal the genuine intensity of his love for her. His remorseful misery was not a fully orchestrated performance like that of Queen Victoria following Prince Albert's death, yet, after its own private fashion, the quality of his loss was no less authentic. The ache of loneliness was certainly not to be solaced by Elizabeth Villiers, now discreetly sent packing with a large financial settlement, or by a new Dutch favourite, Arnold Joost van Keppel, whose striking good looks set scabrous tongues wagging and whose bumptious opportunism put the loyal Hans Willem Bentinck's nose decidedly out of joint.

A touch of rival's malice infused Bentinck's warning to William that rumour mills were grinding overtime with 'things I am ashamed to hear and from which I believe you to be as far removed as any man in the world'. The king, catching his drift at once, but equally alert to Bentinck's wounded feelings, distanced himself from 'such horrible calumnies' with assurances that 'it is impossible to love you more perfectly than I do'.[25] Keppel, as confidently heterosexual as Bentinck (though rather more disreputably so), remained intimate with William for the rest of his reign, the king cherishing each without managing to bring them together as friends. Gossip as to his own sexuality, if he knew of it, seems never to have troubled him, simply because there was nothing in this respect that he could wish to conceal.

The perfect consolation prize for Bentinck, now Duke of Portland, was as plenipotentiary for the peace negotiations with France, concluded in 1697 at the Dutch town of Rijswijk near Delft and known to British history as 'the Treaty of Ryswick'. The agreement was a triumph for Bentinck's diplomacy – Louis was massively impressed by his urbanity, fashionable clothes and flawless politesse – and for William's international alliance. His policy of resistance to Louis whatever the cost had substantially succeeded, France had been forced into major strategic and economic concessions and England could now step forward to assume the role of a major European power, which it would validate for the next two hundred and fifty years, until the end of the Second World War. Louis agreed, what is more, to recognize William as King of England and, while setting aside a demand that James be obliged to quit France, he promised 'not to assist, directly or indirectly, the enemies of M le Prince d'Orange'.[26]

Among the princes of Europe, William's personal stock had risen as the course of the recent war revealed his gifts for the leadership of an international army and for concentrating his fractious, not always dependable alliance on the operational tasks in hand. 'Everywhere you hear people say "He is a man of genius – a great King and worthy to be so",' noted Liselotte d'Orléans.[27] Receiving news of his safety following yet another Jacobite assassination plot, King Carl of Sweden and his ministers drank exultant healths to William, the Duke of Hesse-Kassel ordered a Te Deum to be sung and the nuns of Brussels said prayers in their convents. In France, according to the diplomat-poet

Matthew Prior, accompanying Bentinck's embassy, 'it is incredible what true respect and veneration they bear to King William . . . and how the soldiers particularly speak of him. "*Le premier homme de son métier*"! "*Le plus beau prince du monde!*"'[28]

Conspicuously lacking in vanity, William appeared indifferent to such adulation. Within his own kingdom, as he well knew, it was a good deal less forthcoming and likely to diminish still further as peacetime conditions made him seem, all of a sudden, oddly superfluous to the nation's affairs. The closing years of his reign were soured by resentment and hostility between his ministers, amid a general feeling that he had exploited their goodwill throughout the war while heaping too many honours and gifts on his Dutch favourites. Parliament, as the new political genie released from the bottle, now tackled with relish its role of keeping the monarch firmly in check, rejecting his demand for a standing army, refusing to allow Huguenot refugees to settle in Ireland, blocking his attempt to bring the English calendar into line with the continent's, and obstructing his plans for a full union between the English and Scottish crowns.

Equally venomous was the opposition by the parliament in Dublin to William's generous treatment of Irish Catholics in the articles of the Treaty of Limerick, concluded in 1691 but still unratified six years later, whose terms promised to cancel outlawries and forfeitures against them and restore the favourable conditions under which they had lived during Charles II's reign. William had dismissed, what is more, a preposterous demand by Church of Ireland bishops for the banishment of all popish clergy, and assured Emperor Leopold of Austria that he would do his best for the Catholic population in Ireland. He was somewhat less inclined to do this when, after the Treaty of Ryswick's territorial reassignments, Leopold and Louis began a combined harassment of Protestants in Alsace and eastern France. Defeated in any case over the Limerick provisions, William received a further snub from his English parliament when it refused to grant the crown its customary one-third share of forfeited estates, certain MPs throwing in for good measure, during debate on the issue, a number of off-colour remarks on the king as a private individual. Among the Irish Catholics themselves, however, William's name was not always reviled, if only because his policy of religious moderation meant that they would endure no further wholesale persecution under official auspices, and the severity of the penal laws depended on those applying them.

Scotland provided another source of worry altogether. Responsibility for the 1692 Glencoe massacre, in which a delay by the Highland clan Macdonald in taking its oath of loyalty to the king by an appointed day was invoked as an excuse for slaughter by its ancient enemies the clan Campbell, is routinely laid at William's door by bleeding-heart Scots nationalists. The notorious order 'to extirpate that set of thieves'[29] formulated by secretary of state John Dalrymple, Master of Stair, was countersigned by the king on the basis of false information. When, however, a subsequent inquiry ordered by William found Stair guilty of instigating what was effectively an act of tribal mass murder under judicial sanction, the former declined to administer a punishment many in Scotland felt the crafty Edinburgh lawyer amply deserved.

William's enduring neglect of his northern kingdom – he never set foot there throughout his reign – raised justifiable resentment among the Scots, exacerbated by the disastrous failure in the late 1690s of the colonial project in Panama known as the Darien Scheme, a Scottish attempt at gaining economic independence from England. The government in London was seen as arrogant, bullying and greedy, to the extent that open warfare between the two realms became a not inconceivable scenario. It was William's own solution, basically a counsel of despair, that of uniting the two crowns (something proposed nearly a hundred years earlier by his great-grandfather King James I but rejected by the English parliament), which became a constitutional reality soon after his death. The 1707 Act of Union fulfilled, in effect, his glumly practical scissors-and-paste approach to a problem of nationhood which, through his own distaste for certain important aspects of the hands-on business of kingship, he had surely helped to create.

The feeling of disjunction between William and his unruly realm grew marked during 1700–1701, the last two years of his reign. As Parliament tore itself to shreds through factionalism, plots and counterplots, name-calling and denunciation, he seems genuinely to have pondered the likelihood of quitting for good what, in a fit of angry disgust, he had called 'ce vilain pays', to spend the rest of his days in Holland. He could be happy at Het Loo, with memories of Mary, his collection of choice Dutch and Italian paintings and more gardens to plan. Among the few consolations life in London afforded was his little nephew William Henry, Duke of Gloucester, son of Princess Anne, with whom, after Mary's death, some attempt was made at fence-mending. The precocious prince, now William's heir, had dedicated himself to his uncle's service and the king delighted to foster the boy's soldiership with a miniature guards regiment marching to a band of oboes. When Gloucester, suffering from water on the brain, died, aged only eleven, William grieved as if for his own son.

Through Gloucester's death the Protestant succession, central to the Revolution settlement, was now endangered, but it was over rival claims by France and Austria to the kingdom of Spain and its vast American trading empire that England was drawn into war once again. A new decade of conflict would follow, from which the post-1707 United Kingdom of Great Britain emerged yet more potent and predominant, its naval supremacy over world trade routes guaranteed, its international prestige immeasurably enhanced. William would not live to witness this triumph. In despair over Parliament's parochial intransigence as France broke the Ryswick treaty terms to consolidate its Bourbon claim to the Spanish throne, he was oppressed by constant illness – fever, asthma, shingles and stomach pains – suggesting a further breakdown of an already weakened immune system. The sick king faced his Lords and Commons for the last time on 31 December 1701. By now an Act of Settlement had secured Anne as his successor and after her the Protestant house of Hanover. England, renewing its alliance with Austria and the Dutch, had opened hostilities with France in the War of the Spanish Succession.

William's warning to Parliament 'to lay aside those unhappy fatal animosities which divide and weaken you' was timely enough. How seriously his assurance 'It is and always has been my desire to be the common father of my people' was taken we cannot know.[30]

Early in the New Year, while riding in the park at Hampton Court, he was thrown from his horse when it stumbled on a molehill. A broken collarbone might have mended easily but a few days later he caught a severe chill, which turned into pneumonia, and knew that the end was upon him. As courtiers gathered for another royal deathbed, William, despite being so close to death, showed 'a clear and full presence of mind, and a wonderful tranquillity'.[31] In his last moments he ordered Bentinck to be summoned. Pressing his friend's hand to his heart with a sigh, he died. When his body was undressed for burial, a ring containing a lock of Mary's hair was found tied around his left arm.

5
Epilogue

England forgot William and Mary easily enough. Anne, as their successor, even if she did not indulge in the Roman imperial exercise of *damnatio memoriae*, which involved expunging all official traces of a particularly obnoxious forerunner, was hardly going to perform more than the customary decency required in paying funeral honours to two individuals she had no special cause to love. Though Protestant Ireland kept alive its selective anti-papist image of William the Deliverer, he only re-emerged for the English at moments when it seemed they needed reminding of the reasons why their freedom and prosperity were notionally greater than those of other European nations. Thomas Babington Macaulay, doyen of Victorian Whig champions of the Glorious Revolution, fashioned a heroic figure from the Prince of Orange, downplaying Mary's contribution to the joint reign and making each of them, in the process, a hostage to fortune. The Dutchman and his queen took their places among the worthies in that version of history whose successive chapters moved in Darwinian evolutionary sequence towards Great Britain's state of seamless perfection as a torchbearer of liberty, democracy and progress.

This Whig theory of history became an obvious target

for revisionists, making easy casualties out of William and Mary in the process. Neither of them would ever be a popular subject for biographers. William's essential reserve and secretiveness, not to speak of the fact that much of the early source material for his life was in Dutch, made him unappealing to anglophone historians. Mary proved still less engaging. What sort of narrative heroine could be made from a woman whose short life was so conspicuously virtuous – apart from her quarrel with Anne and the Marlboroughs, where there were faults on both sides – and whose anguished Protestant piety precluded any sort of scandal?

This was indeed the problem with England's sovereign double act – not enough high-end gossip and sleaze. Their reign effectively killed off the world of the Restoration, with its duels and debauches, its gropers and fumblers, whores and orange-wenches, clap-doctors, cuckolds, rogues and bullies. Part of the trouble with William and Mary, for succeeding generations, has been that they were too seriously respectable. He was his wife's only love and she had no interest in dalliance or casual flirtation. Hard evidence is lacking, meanwhile, for William's supposed sodomy with Bentinck and Keppel, while Elizabeth Villiers always played things cool as a royal attachment, never seeking to embarrass the king or upstage the queen.

The palaces they created at Kensington, Hampton Court and Het Loo were carefully designed domestic spaces which underscored the dignity and good behaviour of their owners and those attending on them. At the same time, such buildings and their gardens guaranteed the chance for privacy, for the grateful embrace of that occasional solitariness vital to William and Mary's survival as individuals coping with the wearying burden of kingship. The extensive destruction by fire of the rambling old palace of Whitehall in 1698 can thus be seen as inherently symbolic. William had never cared for it and his chief anxiety now was for the fate of the art works it contained. No serious attempt at rebuilding was ever made. The place, after all, enshrined a dead, or at least moribund, construct of royalty as a fulcrum of patronage and influence. Court culture, that nirvana for the ambitious and aspirational under earlier Stuart kings, with the monarch on display at the centre of a continuous public theatre composed of levees, banquets, masques, balls, hunts and progresses, slowly but perceptibly lost its centrality and allure.

Such a shift in emphasis was due not solely to the wholesale shake-up of national governance after the Revolution. It owed much to the personal scruples and priorities of the two sovereigns themselves. Each understood how essential to the monarchy's survival was the recovery of that decorum lost under King Charles II. Mary contributed to this process more than is sometimes acknowledged, through the instinctive grasp of her role as a public example. However much her cynicism was sharpened by bitter experience, she continued to demand good conduct and moral probity from others, even if she doubted they could rise to the challenge. She was intensely patriotic, making England's honour a matter of vital concern. The realization of her project for a sailors' hospital at Greenwich is a tribute to this impulse, one of those charitable initiatives which drew praise even

from those who contested her right to the crown. The Jacobite Lord Ailesbury, whom she had saved from execution,
called her 'that great princess', a woman whose 'humanity
was without example'. He understood, what was more, the
profound misgiving with which she faced her royal duties
and seems to have appreciated the inherent emotional conflict underlying her marriage to William: 'Whether she had
good returns I question much ... She submitted, but God
knows what she suffered inwardly, and to a high degree.'[1]

Mary's maternal grandfather, the politician and historian
Lord Clarendon, writing of Oliver Cromwell, described
him (borrowing a quotation from Pliny the Younger) as a
man whom his enemies, though they might not praise,
could not wholly condemn.[2] Of King William III the same
was true and in his case several of those we might have
expected to hate him were surprisingly generous in their
praise. James II's bastard son the Duke of Berwick, a
gallant commander of French troops in Flanders, acknowledged: 'I cannot deny him the character of a great man and
even of a great king.'[3] Even the Sultan of Turkey, sworn foe
of Christian monarchs, saluted William as 'this most glorious of the great princes of the prophet Jesus'.[4] However
intimidating his habitual reserve, he was a king who
inspired genuine respect and devotion among those who
managed to get close to him. 'Condescending without
meanness, courteous without fawning and grave without
moroseness,' recalled one of them, 'as compleat a Gentle-
man as ever Europe had to boast of.'[5]

By the very nature of his ascent to the throne, William
was – we had better add a dutiful 'perhaps' here – the only

English monarch not to take for granted the rights and privileges considered due to him simply as a result of his royal birth. He had refused to accept the crown as a trophy of conquest, wisely receiving it instead from Parliament's hands with all the implied limitations on his prerogative. If the rule of law, so often invoked as a cornerstone of English freedom, did not begin with William, then he contributed towards cementing it within the civic life of the state. Initially a bill designed to guarantee the independence of the judiciary had proposed that judges' salaries be paid from the Civil List. This was understandably vetoed by the king as a drain on his already stretched personal resources. He continued, however, unlike Charles II and James II, to respect the liberty of his judges, underwritten by the 1701 Act of Settlement, which declared that 'the Laws of England are the Birthright of the People thereof'.[6]

Such ideas were canvassed more freely after 1695, when Parliament abandoned the licensing of printed books, pamphlets and newspapers. Though sedition could still be punished with a spell in the pillory, public opinion was effectively set free, political and religious issues could be examined and commented on without fear of prosecution and the nation developed an insatiable appetite for newsprint as local papers sprang up across England. Changes like these give William and Mary the right to be considered the first sovereigns of modern England and make the 1690s a decade of crucial significance in the history of the Western world. It was an age when witchcraft trials were discredited, when the right of black African slaves to liberty on English soil was first asserted by a Lord Chief Justice and when a freethinker like John Toland could publish a book entitled *Christianity not Mysterious* without fearing that either it or the publisher or he himself would be burnt for such audacity.

Of our two monarchs Mary is obviously the easier to love, yet in writing this book I've learned why those closest to him became unshakeably attached to William. He had his moments of glacial remoteness, his fits of bad temper, his occasional cheese-paring parsimony, but he was the only Stuart king whose word of honour it was possible to trust, who was never vindictive and in whom a mature awareness of his royal responsibility took pride of place over his sense of personal entitlement. Absolutist by inclination though he certainly was, he quickly grasped the hard truth that among the English he would never have the chance to emulate his cousin Louis XIV and that there was no point in trying to do so. His achievement, with Mary beside him, was to demonstrate to England how monarchy could work effectively as an integral component of the nation's wider constitutional equilibrium. Modest, grown-up creatures of common sense, William and Mary were a far better king and queen than their subjects honestly deserved.

Notes

1. CHILDREN OF STATE

1. *Hamlet*, I.iii.17–24.
2. Andrew Marvell, 'An Horatian Ode upon Cromwell's Return from Ireland' (1650).
3. Quoted in Pieter Geyl, *Orange and Stuart 1641–1672* (London: Weidenfeld & Nicolson, 1969), p. 129.
4. Stephen B. Baxter, *William III* (London: Longman, 1966), p. 4.
5. *The Diary of Samuel Pepys*, ed. Robert Latham and William Matthews (London: G. Bell, 1970), vol. 1, p. 261, entry for 7 October 1660.
6. Gilbert Burnet, *Bishop Burnet's History of His Own Time*, 2nd edn (Oxford: 1833), vol. 1, p. 303.
7. Edward Hyde, Earl of Clarendon, *The Life of Edward Earl of Clarendon* (Oxford: Clarendon Press, 1827), vol. 1, p. 401.
8. *Diary of Samuel Pepys*, vol. 3, p. 75, entry for 1 May 1662.
9. Quoted in Hester W. Chapman, *Mary II, Queen of England* (London: Jonathan Cape, 1953), p. 55.
10. Sir William Temple, *The Works of Sir William Temple, Bart.* (London: F. C. and J. Rivington, 1814), vol. 2, pp. 343–4.
11. 'Diary of Dr Edward Lake', ed. G. P. Elliott, p. 5, entry for 21 October 1677, in *Camden Miscellany*, vol. 1, Camden Society, Old Series, 39 (London: 1847), p. 5.
12. Burnet, *Bishop Burnet's History*, p. 272.
13. Quoted in Nesca A. Robb, *William of Orange: A Personal Portrait*, vol. 2 (London: Heinemann, 1966), p. 99.

2. THE PROTESTANT WIND

1. Quoted in Chapman, *Mary II*, p. 126.
2. Burnet, *Bishop Burnet's History*, vol. 3, p. 133.
3. N. Japikse (ed.), *Correspondentie van Willem III en van Hans Willem Bentinck* (The Hague: Martinus Nijhoff, 1927–37), part 1, vol. 1, p. 9, quoted in Robb, *William of Orange*, p. 139.
4. *The Correspondence of Henry Hyde, Earl of Clarendon*, ed. S. W. Singer (London: Henry Colburn, 1828), vol. 1, pp. 37–8.
5. Burnet, *Bishop Burnet's History*, vol. 3, p. 133.

6. Patrick Hume, 'Memorial upon the Edict in Scotland of 12th February 1687', sent by Hume to Prince William of Orange (*c.* 2 May 1687), quoted in Baxter, *William III*, p. 220.

7. *Hamlet*, V.ii.380–81.

8. *Correspondence of Henry Hyde*, vol. 2, p. 156.

9. Sir John Dalrymple, *Memoirs of Great Britain and Ireland*, 2nd edn (London: 1773), vol. 2, p. 313.

10. Temple, *Works of Sir William Temple*, vol. 4, p. 326.

11. Quoted in Baxter, *William III*, p. 225.

12. Burnet, *Bishop Burnet's History*, vol. 3, p. 260.

13. Dalrymple, *Memoirs*, p. 303–4. Mary's questionnaire is quoted in Chapman, *Mary II*, pp. 263–6.

14. *London Gazette*, no. 2386 (27 September–1 October 1688), quoted in Tim Harris, *Revolution: The Great Crisis of the British Monarchy, 1685–1720* (London: Allen Lane, 2006), p. 277.

15. British Library, Add. MS 4163.

16. Mechtilde, Comtesse Bentinck, *Lettres et mémoires de Marie II* (The Hague: 1880), pp. 80–88, quoted in Chapman, *Mary II*, p. 149.

17. Ibid.

18. Ibid.

19. Quoted in Robb, *William of Orange*, p. 265.

20. John Whittle, *An Exact Diary of the Late Expedition of His Illustrious Highness the Prince of Orange* (London: Richard Baldwin, 1689), p. 19.

21. Quoted in Chapman, *Mary II*, p. 151.

22. Burnet, *Bishop Burnet's History*, vol. 3, p. 328.

23. *The Diary of John Evelyn* (London: Dent, 1907), vol. 2, pp. 284–5, entry for 14 October 1688.

3. MONARCHY BY CONTRACT

1. *Measure for Measure*, I.i.68–73.

2. Sarah Churchill, *An Account of the Conduct of the Dowager Duchess of Marlborough* (London: George Hawkins, 1742), p. 26.

3. *Diary of John Evelyn*, vol. 2, p. 294, entry for 21 February 1689.

4. Adapted from Burnet, *Bishop Burnet's History*, vol. 3, p. 396 n⁰.

5. Adapted from ibid., p. 393.

6. Jacobus Scheltema, *Geschied- en letterkundig mengelwerk*, vol. 2 (Amsterdam: H. Gartman, 1817), p. 184, quoted in Robb, *William of Orange*, p. 288.

7. Japikse (ed.), *Correspondentie*, part 2, vol. 3, p. 102.

8. R. Doebner (ed.), *Memoirs of Mary, Queen of England* (London: D. Nutt, 1886), p. 11.

9. *Hamlet*, IV.v.120.

10. Anchitell Grey, *Debates of the House of Commons, From the Year 1667 to the Year 1694* (London: 1769), vol. 9, pp. 25, 29.

11. John Locke, letter to Philippus van Limborch, 6 June 1689, *The Correspondence of John Locke*, ed. E. S. de Beer, vol. 3 (Oxford: Clarendon Press, 1978), p. 633.

12. Pádraig Lenihan, *1690: Battle of the Boyne* (Stroud: History Press, 2003), p. 272.

13. Doebner (ed.), *Memoirs of Mary*, p. 14.

14. Quoted in Lenihan, *1690*, p. 71.
15. Historical Manuscripts Commission, *Report on the Manuscripts of the Late Allan George Finch, Esq., of Burley-on-the-Hill, Rutland*, vol. 2 (London: HMSO, 1922), p. 326.
16. *Notes & Queries*, 5th Series, vol. 8, p. 21.
17. Historical Manuscripts Commission, *Report on the Manuscripts of the Late Allan George Finch*, p. 330.
18. Doebner (ed.), *Memoirs of Mary*, p. 29.
19. Ibid., p. 30.
20. Quoted in Chapman, *Mary II*, pp. 180–81.
21. *Diary of John Evelyn*, vol. 2, p. 305, entry for 25 February 1690.

4. A LONELY CROWN

1. *Journals of the House of Lords*, vol. 14 (1685–91), p. 320.
2. Ibid., p. 128.
3. Doebner (ed.), *Memoirs of Mary*, p. 59.
4. Anonymous contemporary broadsheet, quoted in Chapman, *Mary II*, p. 233.
5. *London Gazette*, no. 2767 (16–19 May 1692).
6. William Anderton, *Remarks upon the Present Confederacy, and Late Revolution in England* (London: 1693).
7. Gilbert Burnet, *A Supplement to Burnet's History of My Own Time*, ed. H. C. Foxcroft (Oxford: Clarendon Press, 1902), p. 373.
8. Thomas Birch, *The Life of Archbishop Tillotson* (London: 1752), p. 281.
9. Quoted in Chapman, *Mary II*, p. 225.
10. Doebner (ed.), *Memoirs of Mary*, p. 54.
11. Ibid., p. 55.
12. W. E. Buckley (ed.), *Memoirs of Thomas, Earl of Ailesbury, Written by Himself* (London: Nichols and Son, 1890), vol. 1, p. 298, with reference to Ezekiel 37:3: 'And [the Lord] said unto me, Son of man, can these [dry] bones live?'
13. Sir John Hawkins, *A General History of the Science and Practice of Music* (London: Novello, Ewer & Co., 1875), vol. 2, p. 564 n*.
14. Burnet, *Bishop Burnet's History*, vol. 4, p. 249 n.
15. Adapted from ibid., pp. 246–7.
16. Ibid., p. 247.
17. James Ralph, *The History of England* (London: Waller, 1746), vol. 2, p. 540.
18. *Diary of John Evelyn*, vol. 2, p. 336, entry for 8 March 1695.
19. Ibid., pp. 335–6, entry for 5 March 1695.
20. Quoted in Christopher Hogwood, 'Thomas Tudway's History of Music', in Christopher Hogwood and Richard Luckett (eds), *Music in Eighteenth-Century England* (Cambridge: Cambridge University Press, 1983), p. 28.
21. *Diary of John Evelyn*, vol. 2, p. 336, entry for 8 March 1695.
22. John Oldmixon, *The History of England during the Reigns of the King William and Queen Mary, Queen Anne, King George I* (London: 1735), p. 96, with reference to II Kings 9:34.
23. Quoted in Mary Hopkirk, *The Queen Over the Water: Mary Beatrice of Modena, Queen of James II* (London: John Murray, 1953), p. 167.

24. Japikse (ed.), *Correspondentie*, part 2, vol. 1, p. 347.
25. Ibid., part 1, vol. 1, pp. 199, 200, 202.
26. Quoted in Baxter, *William III*, p. 356.
27. *Correspondance complète de madame duchesse d'Orléans*, ed. Ernest Jaeglé (Paris: Charpentier, 1886), vol. 1, p. 130, quoted in Robb, *William of Orange*, p. 375.
28. Historical Manuscripts Commission, *Calendar of the Manuscripts of the Marquis of Bath Preserved at Longleat, Wiltshire* (London: HMSO, 1908), vol. 3, p. 278.
29. Quoted in Baxter, *William III*, p. 273.
30. Quoted in Robb, *William of Orange*, p. 477.
31. Burnet, *Bishop Burnet's History*, vol. 4, p. 561.

5. EPILOGUE

1. W. E. Buckley (ed.), *Memoirs of Thomas, Earl of Ailesbury*, vol. 1, p. 299.
2. Edward Hyde, Earl of Clarendon, *The History of the Rebellion and Civil Wars in England* (Oxford: Clarendon Press, 1826), vol. 7, p. 293, with reference to Pliny the Younger, *Letters* III.12.4.
3. Quoted in Robb, *William of Orange*, p. 497.
4. Quoted in ibid., p. 490.
5. Quoted in ibid., p. 498.
6. Act of Settlement (1700), 12 & 13 Will. III, c. 2.

Further Reading

For different reasons, William and Mary have never been popular subjects for biographers. The most comprehensive view of William as a private individual remains Nesca A. Robb's two-volume study *William of Orange: A Personal Portrait* (London: Heinemann, 1962 and 1966), based on Dutch and English sources. Though Robb is evidently more than a little in love with her subject – not necessarily a bad thing in a biographer – she makes an excellent case for that greatness accorded him by his contemporaries. A more detached account of his achievement in the context of history, English, Dutch or European, is afforded by Stephen B. Baxter's *William III* (London: Longman, 1966), regarded as the standard professional biography, though perhaps less enjoyable than Robb's from the aspect of narrative detail. An outstanding study of William's political career in the Netherlands and England is Tony Claydon's *William III* (London: Longman, 2002). This lucid, carefully balanced assessment of the monarch's contribution towards the making of the modern British state within his three kingdoms plausibly proposes William's foreignness, whether in origin or outlook, as one of the reasons why the English never took him to their hearts. Of Mary only a single life exists. Hester W. Chapman's *Mary II, Queen of England* (London: Jonathan Cape, 1953) may seem old-fashioned in style and not without occasional touches of that pernicious French hybrid *la biographie romancée*, but it offers a well-researched and exceedingly penetrating portrait of Mary as both woman and sovereign. Chapman's empathy with the period in general is a further asset in a book which deserves a reissue. On the Glorious Revolution, Tim Harris's *Revolution: The Great Crisis of the British Monarchy, 1685–1720* (London: Allen Lane, 2006) and Steve Pincus's *1688: The First Modern Revolution* (New Haven, Conn., and London: Yale

University Press, 2009) can both be recommended. The former surveys the impact of the Revolution across Britain, with a significant focus on events in Scotland and Ireland. The latter makes a convincing case for viewing the whole episode as ultimately more important than the French Revolution in the history of the modern world. Edward Vallance's *The Glorious Revolution: 1688 – Britain's Fight for Liberty* (London: Little, Brown, 2006) presents a reliable narrative account of what happened and why. No separate study exists of the so-called Nine Years War of 1688–97. William's military career is partially outlined in John Childs's *The Williamite Wars in Ireland, 1688–1691* (London: Continuum, 2007) and the sea battles are covered by Edward B. Powley's *The Naval Side of King William's War* (London: John Baker, 1972). Pádraig Lenihan's *1690: Battle of the Boyne* (Stroud: History Press, 2003) offers a modern Irish perspective on the battle, its context and long-term results. Where William himself is concerned, the writer's attitude does not transcend traditional prejudices. Political and religious dimensions of William and Mary's reign are examined by a range of authoritative contributors to *Britain After the Glorious Revolution, 1689–1714*, edited by Geoffrey Holmes (London: Macmillan, 1969). A wider historical conspectus is offered in the relevant chapters of Julian Hoppit's *A Land of Liberty? England 1689–1727* (Oxford: Oxford University Press, 2000), part of the New Oxford History of England series. Pieter Geyl's *Orange and Stuart 1641–1672* (London: Weidenfeld & Nicolson, 1969), translated by Arnold Pomerans from the original Dutch edition of 1939, provides a valuable background perspective to William's Anglo-Dutch boyhood and youth. A Jacobite perspective on the Revolution and its aftermath is provided by Mary Hopkirk's *The Queen Over the Water: Mary Beatrice of Modena, Queen of James II* (London: John Murray, 1953). There is no worthwhile historical fiction set during this period. The action of Peter Greenaway's much-admired film *The Draughtsman's Contract* (1982) is located (with several deliberate anachronisms, including a cordless phone and a painting by Roy Lichtenstein) within an authentic enough atmosphere of arriviste prosperity in 1694. Nobody, so far as I can tell, has ever tried to write a play, an opera or a ballet about William and Mary. Such an exercise might repay the effort involved.

Picture Credits

1. Adriaen Hanneman, portrait of William III when Prince of Orange, as a child, 1654 (© Rijksmuseum, Amsterdam)
2. Sir Peter Lely, the Princess Mary, detail from a portrait of James II, when Duke of York, with Anne Hyde, Princess Mary and Princess Anne, *c.*1668–85 (Royal Collection Trust © Her Majesty Queen Elizabeth II, 2014/Bridgeman Images)
3. William Wissing, portrait of William III when Prince of Orange, *c.*1670 (private collection/© Philip Mould Ltd, London/Bridgeman Images)
4. Sir Peter Lely, portrait of Mary II as Princess of Orange, 1677 (GL Archive/Alamy)
5. Anon., *The Protestant Grind-Stone*, *c.*1690 (Universal History Archive/UIG Bridgeman Images)
6. Jan Wyck, *William of Orange at the Battle of the Boyne*, 1690 (Mount Stewart House & Garden, County Down, Northern Ireland/National Trust Photographic Library/Bridgeman Images)
7. Godfried Schalcken, portrait of William III, *c.*1692–7 (© Rijksmuseum, Amsterdam)
8. Sir Godfrey Kneller, portrait of Mary II (detail), 1690 (The Royal Collection Trust © Her Majesty Queen Elizabeth II, 2014/Bridgeman Images)
9. Godfrey Kneller (after), portrait of Queen Anne and William Henry, Duke of Gloucester, *c.*1694 (National Portrait Gallery, London/Bridgeman Images)
10. Leonard Knyff, *A View of Hampton Court* (detail), *c.*1702 (The Royal Collection Trust © Her Majesty Queen Elizabeth II, 2014/Bridgeman Images)

Index